MW01408833

STRIKE 3

WHAT TO DO WHEN THE GAME'S OVER . . .
BUT LIFE IS NOT

JOSHUA KALINOWSKI

Copyright © 2020 Joshua Kalinowski

All rights reserved. No part of this book may be used or reproduced in any manner whatsoever without prior written consent of the authors, except as provided by the United States of America copyright law.

Published by Best Seller Publishing®, Pasadena, CA
Best Seller Publishing® is a registered trademark
Printed in the United States of America.

ISBN: 978-1949535785

This publication is designed to provide accurate and authoritative information with regard to the subject matter covered. It is sold with the understanding that the publisher is not engaged in rendering legal, accounting, or other professional advice. If legal advice or other expert assistance is required, the services of a competent professional should be sought. The opinions expressed by the authors in this book are not endorsed by Best Seller Publishing® and are the sole responsibility of the author rendering the opinion.

For more information, please write:

Best Seller Publishing®
253 N. San Gabriel Blvd, Unit B
Pasadena, CA 91107
or call 1 (626) 765 9750

Visit us online at: www.BestSellerPublishing.org

Contents

Foreword vii

Introduction 1

Chapter 1: Greatness Escaped 9
   Forever Chasing 11
   My Outside Didn't Match My Insides 14
   What's Your New Superpower? 17

Chapter 2: The Chase 21
   Trust Your Team 23
   Rebar 25
   The Notion We All Have Greatness within Is a Lie 26
   Integrity Moments 30
   Too Good to Be True 32
   After the Game Is Over 35

Chapter 3: Be the Inspiration You Need 39
   Forgiving the Debt 41
   Move Your Finish Line 43

Chapter 4: Soul Search 47
    Passion vs. Purpose 47
    Dream and Search—Repeat 48
    Your Purpose 50
    Face the Storm 51
    Clarity 53

Chapter 5: Forgiving the Failure 55
    The Weight of Shadows 55
    Taming the Beast 57
    The Right Relationship 59
    We Are All Broken 60
    Taking Ownership 61
    A Door of Possibility 64
    Knocking Down Your Walls 65

Chapter 6: Power of Presence 67
    Search Mission 67
    Authority 68
    Never Again 70
    Two Beasts 71
    Tell the Truth 73
    Take Back the 1% 74

Chapter 7: Impact & Influence 79
    Qualified by Failure 79
    The Formula 80
    Wisdom, Knowledge, and Understanding 82
    Our Stories 86

Chapter 8: Finding Your Team 89
   You Are Not Alone 89
   Coming Clean 91
   It's Possible 94

Chapter 9: Swing Batter, Batter 95
   From Paralysis to Peace 95
   No One Is Coming to Save You 96
   Developing Yourself 96
   Fill Your Cups 97
   Pour into Others 99

Chapter 10: Casting Your Vision 103
   What Is the Price? 103
   A Vision for Your Life 106
   Your Story Is Yours 107

Chapter 11: Designed through Failure 109
   You Have One Life to Live 109
   The True Game 110
   Be More 111
   Give It Your All 113

Draw the Line in the Sand 117
   There Is No One Thing 118

Acknowledgment 125

Foreword

I was really hungry.
It had been three days since my last meal. That is, if you count extremely flat Mug Root Beer as a meal.

Even though this happened over 24 years ago, I remember this day like it was yesterday.

The interesting thing was that my friends and family thought that I was living the dream.

My parents had made the ultimate sacrifice of selling almost all of their worldly possessions to send me, their ambitious and rebellious teenager, from the streets of India to have a better life in the United States. My high school friends were equal parts impressed and envious that I was able to escape the hood forever and that I was going to study at some fancy college in the US.

But my temporary reality was a little different.

It was my first week in a small town in rural Iowa and nobody seemed to understand my accent-infused English. The hundred and twenty odd dollars of cash that my parents had given me when I boarded the flight had run out after traveling 9,000 miles half-way across the world. The international check that my parents had given me for a year's worth of expenses needed another 7-10 days to clear and transfer into my account.

Which brings me back to not having had a meal in 3 days.

I had crashed every pizza party that I could and drank more root beer than anyone should in a year, let alone a week. It would suffice it to say I had made the "not welcome" list for any and every campus party, fraternity rush—even the chess club's welcome social.

All I really needed was a meal… not just for physical sustenance but to also get my mind right.

I heard there was a soup kitchen somewhere in town so I went searching for it. I walked for miles looking for it. I got totally lost and I had no courage to ask anyone for directions. What was I going to say to a random stranger? "Hello Ma'am… can you tell me where I can go get some free food?"

No. That would have been ultra-awkward for both of us.

After walking for hours, I was tired and I couldn't find the soup kitchen. So, I turned around and walked back to campus.

It was already dark. I was exhausted. And I was starting to get depressed.

That's when I walked by a dumpster and saw two guys throwing stuff away. While I couldn't clearly see all the trash that they were throwing away, one thing was absolutely unmistakable: a large pizza box.

At that moment, I would have traded you all my possessions for a few slices of cold pepperoni pizza.

As soon as the guys left, I made my way to the dumpster and instinct took over.

I jumped in. Grabbed the pizza box. Jumped out.

And ran like a bat out of hell.

I found myself a spot on a park bench and I opened the box to find two slices of leftover pizza with parts of the crust nibbled off. I didn't care. I scarfed them down.

Right then was a moment that I will never forget. A moment where I felt the strangest emotions I had ever felt before. I felt shame. I felt unworthiness. And worst of all, I felt totally alone.

Now you must be thinking: what does this story have to do with this book?

Here's the answer: *Everything makes sense when someone gives you the answer.*

When things don't go our way, we can feel like it's "game over" and the hardest part is knowing what to do when it is over but life's not.

Yes, it was a rough situation:

- I was sixteen years old
- I was broke
- I didn't know where my next meal was going to come from
- I had no friends
- I couldn't communicate with anyone
- I was scared
- I was ashamed
- I was alone
- And I had no idea when anything was going to get better

I felt like life was game over before it had even begun.

And after I read the first draft of this book, I wished I could have given this book to my 16 year old self when he was dumpster diving for leftover pizza to remind him that "game over" only means that *this* game is over, and there's another one coming. "Game over" means I get to play again. It means I will get more chances to win. It also means I will get more chances to lose.

But how do you know what to do when the game's over, but life is not?

From dumpster diving in rural Iowa, to having 5 exits in the last 20 years, to building companies with hundreds of employees and billions of dollars in sales, to unimaginable experiences from Wall Street to Beverly Hills, and from Dubai to Silicon Valley, one thing never changes: the emotional rollercoaster of it all.

This book is your answer to the emotional rollercoaster of life, love and business.

This book is your inner support system to understand what to do when the game's over, but life is not.

I am intentionally calling this your inner support system not only because of the advice, perspective and wisdom these pages will give you, but more importantly because the person who wrote this book thoughtfully stitched every single sentence together in service of you.

The first time I met Josh Kalinowski, I knew that I was going to be friends with him forever.

I remember the feeling vividly. It was more than a feeling of utter humility, it was more than respectful warmth, it was more than the spirit of friendship. It was a deep sense of purity.

The kind of purity that you are born with.

There are very few individuals in this world who are born to serve, lead and impact the lives of millions of people. It's almost impossible to have the perfect blend of kindness to serve, courage to lead, and commitment to impact all wrapped into one person. In fact, there is no way to engineer this in someone in a lifetime.

Which is why I believe that Josh was born for this. And while some may call this his destiny, I believe this is more than his destiny. I believe this is his responsibility.

And that's why this is not just a collection of chapters and sections. It's a gift to us all.

You are very lucky to be reading this book right now not only because it's filled with an inspiring story of a professional athlete, lessons from a successful entrepreneur and insights from a devoted husband and loving father. This is the story of a man who has lived through the highest of highs and the lowest of lows of this emotional rollercoaster and wants to give you the roadmap for you to be able to do it better.

While everyone's life is filled with extremely unique circumstances, we are all on this emotional rollercoaster of life.

I hope you have amazing relationships, but there's a good chance there may be some struggles along the way. I hope you have an amazing career, but there's a good chance there will be some bumps in the road. I hope you have amazing health, but there's a good chance that you will have to work through some challenges.

I hope you don't have to deal with a torn labrum, or tough business partnerships, or mountains of credit card debt, or a tough career as a pro athlete.

And I sincerely hope that neither you nor your loved ones ever have to dumpster dive for food.

But one thing I have learned from Josh is that it helps to know what to do when things get tough. It helps to know what to do when the game's over but life is not.

If you are around Josh long enough, you will hear him say a phrase that he lives by which pushes me every day to be a better entrepreneur, a better father, a better husband, a better coach, a better friend and a better human being:

Empty the tank, every day in every way.

Get ready to open your heart as Josh pours into you within the pages of this book.

All the best,
Sharran Srivatsaa

PS: *Before you start, flip to Chapter 7 and copy down the Wisdom Formula on a post-it note. It will be a great guide for you as you read this book and also as you go through the journey of life.*

Sharran Srivatsaa is a 4x Inc. 500 Entrepreneur with 5 exits in the last 19 years.

Most recently, Sharran grew Teles Properties by 10x in 5 years to $3.4 Billion in sales and eventually sold the business to Douglas Elliman. Sharran is a former Goldman Sachs and Credit Suisse banker, a sought after keynote speaker, and angel investor. In addition to mentoring CEOs in his ultra-exclusive Legends Program, Sharran also hosts the top-rated podcast "Business School" and is the creator of the wildly-popular 5am Club call for Entrepreneurs.

Introduction

"My life as a professional baseball player has been full of more changeups and fastballs than I could ever have imagined, but worth every pitch, every no-hitter, and every strikeout. It's been a humbling and amazing journey! I am forever indebted to those who have supported me along the way."

This was it. These are the words I pictured speaking at my retirement ceremony from Major League Baseball. My kids standing next to me along with my wife, Kate, and my parents. I pictured their faces and the emotions of the moment. They would have been so proud of all the accomplishments.

I remember watching Cal Ripken Jr. on his stadium and farewell tour the year he retired. Playing for 21 years was a goal I not only aspired to do, but believed with all my heart, mind, and soul I would accomplish.

As athletes, we know the reality of our sport. Eventually, the game will be over. And much like our death we know not the time nor the circumstance of this event, just that it will happen.

I was preparing for my last start of the year in late August of '98 for the Asheville Tourists, a middle A ball, farm team for the Colorado Rockies. We were in Charleston, South Carolina, facing the River Dogs. It had been a pretty good (albeit long) season. It was my first full season of minor league baseball, and I had learned so many lessons along the way—what seat on the bus to take, which teammates to room with on the road, what nights to go out and when to stay in. I learned the importance of burying your curveball for strike three because leaving it over the plate only leads to trouble! Mostly, however, I came to this conclusion: I had never in my life been closer to "the show," yet I still had a long way to go toward stepping foot on a major league field.

But here's the thing: I knew, I believed, I was certain I would get there! It was my purpose, my calling, my reason for being.

While going through my pre-game ritual, I wasn't sure the game was going to happen. The weather report was calling for rain, and the sky was unbelievable, like nothing this Wyoming kid had ever seen. The air was ominously hot and humid, there was a unique pattern of clouds circling and the sky was lit brilliant green, yellow, and red. Perhaps not what you'd hope to see in tornado country.

Four games remained on our schedule, and though this was my last game of the year to pitch, the close of the season still promised plenty of excitement. When starting pitchers are between starts, we spend certain days in the stands with the radar gun. We chart pitches for both teams' pitchers; it's part of our routine and we love it. This gives us a chance to interact with the other teams pitchers and the fans. More importantly, it gives us time with the attending scouts, we get inside information on big league gossip and which players are being slated to move up.

On the mound that evening, I had a feeling tonight was going to be interesting. I had amassed a mediocre record of 11–10; however, the silver lining of the season was pitching a 20 strikeout-and-shutout performance and logging more than 200 strikeouts. If my gut was any indicator, tonight wasn't going to be good for my numbers. The clouds weren't the only thing that looked threatening.

Statistics are everything to a player. *Especially* when fighting to move up or even hold a position. Statistics are job security. Every run, hit, walk, strikeout, win, and loss means passing go and moving up, or emptying your locker, and having to figure out what the heck your life will be like after getting cut from the lead role of your dream life.

STRIKE THREE

As game time neared I kept thinking, *Man, if I can just go five innings and hold it together, I could possibly get my twelfth win, and have a chance at leading the league in strikeouts.* As a competitor we understand this simple truth, "game time" means "go time," if there's glory to be won, awards to take home, or records to break, I'm all in, I've been this way my entire life. Growing up I had a strong sense of competition. In retrospect, it probably cost me in many other areas of my life, but fighting who we are is a battle we face throughout our lives.

After three innings, the weather wasn't the only thing disturbing me. My bread and butter, my curveball, was worthless. Out of the 200-plus strikeouts during the season, my curveball was my go-to pitch. But every time I threw it, it got laced down the foul line. Luckily, they went foul, but no matter the hitter, they were on it and it was worrying me.

As primarily a two-pitch pitcher, I was suddenly forced to lean on a pitch that had eluded me for the better part of my pitching career—the *changeup*. Since the age of fifteen, I'd been trying to add this pitch to my arsenal and could never dial it in. But tonight, I really needed it. If I was going to survive this outing, I didn't have a choice. After I came to the conclusion that I only needed five innings and had to roll with this, my head started to calm.

Having to rely on a pitch I'd struggled with and nearly feared from the time I started throwing would later become a very important metaphor, in my life. When we are forced to step into uncertainty and let go, we often find the freedom we need to be great.

By the fifth inning, I had tuned my sequencing and was getting into a groove, exchanging the curveball for the changeup. In fact, it started to feel like I could use this pitch again. Maybe this was another breakthrough I needed to get me closer to the big leagues. As I approached the mound again I caught a glimpse of the scoreboard, I was aware I hadn't given up a run, but what I didn't realize was *I hadn't given up a hit!*

I remember walking a couple of batters, which is probably why it didn't feel like anything special. Not surprisingly, my mind went immediately to the fact that the perfect game was already impossible due to the walks. As athletes we are conditioned to always find the problem, to look for flaws, find weakness and expose it.

But what if I could pull off a no-hitter? Hall of Fame pitcher Nolan Ryan notched seven in his career (an MLB record that stands unmatched to this day). The statistic that isn't shared very often, and I believe is a powerful one, was the eighteen two-hitters he threw. It's such an amazing stat because it goes to show how hard a no-hitter is to complete. Many pitchers carry a no-hit bid into the eighth or ninth only to be lost by a base hit. All of that perfection broken up by a single base hit! The odds of throwing a no-hitter are 1 in 1,847 games played. That's 0.00054%! MLB has recorded only 303 no-hitters since 1876. As competitors we don't care about the odds, we've beaten them so far. Let someone else worry about them. As far as I was concerned I was hunting down both his records.

As the fifth inning closed without a hit, I remember asking myself: *If I throw a no-hitter in the minor leagues, would it be counted in my major league stats?* Part of me laughs at the naiveté, yet part of me loves that my young spirit allowed such grandiose thoughts.

We often play the lead role in the life we imagine, which is normal and healthy, but letting that image prop you up on a glass pedestal begs for it being shattered.

I paid close attention to my between-inning routine so I could make sure I repeated everything exactly as the inning before. Baseball players are some of the most superstitious athletes. My rituals were deeply rooted from previous experiences. I tightly gripped them as if they were the keys to my future success. Like holding the seams on our favorite pitch, we always hold on to what we know, and endeavor to control anything and everything within our power.

As the innings continued, I began to feel more connected to the game, in tune with the entire stadium. Outs came and went without even noticing; batters stepped into the box, batters left the box. It was so simple and easy. The catcher and I were synced up like never before, and I trusted him. The game was happening effortlessly, like it was in slow motion. I was in the zone. I didn't realize it at the time, but this "zone" has a name: In his book, *Stealing Fire*, Steven Kotler calls this state of being by its phenomenological name—*flow*—which is defined as the optimal state of consciousness.

Flow is basically when a person enters into a mental state where nothing else matters and they're totally absorbed in the moment—everything else disappears. I was there, every move I made was the right move. The pitches were happening automatically and going right where I aimed. This was a new feeling both for me and my team; I wanted (and prayed) to stay there forever.

The fans started to become aware of the situation. Dugouts became alive and no one dared to sit on the bench. It was standing from this point on! Having gone through the seventh inning, we were now six outs away from realizing this could actually happen. As I stepped out onto the mound, I knew that I just needed to trust my catcher and teammates behind me. I needed to continue stepping into the pitches like I'd done all game. We could do this! There had been some amazing plays from the outfielders and infielders helping put us in this situation. I'd taken two line drives off the chest and couldn't have been more proud to feel that sting!

The third out of the eighth inning went into the books. As I approached the dugout I realized this would be the last inning I'd pitch this season.

Never before had I come close to throwing a no-hitter. Most times, throwing a complete game was out of the picture because I typically threw way too many pitches during the game to ever go much further than the seventh inning. Pitching is extremely hard on the body, particularly the shoulder and elbow. For the past three years I had been battling shoulder fatigue. Too young to know any better I kept pushing myself and burying any possibility of really being hurt. Hell, I had a destiny to chase down!

The next three batters were out before they even stepped into the box. I threw the pitches exactly where they were supposed to go, and that was it. Strike three, game over. The no-hitter was complete.

The dugout cleared to rush the mound. My teammates in the field buried us. There was an overwhelming emotion of a greater conviction that overcame me. This *was* my destiny; it was now just a matter of time. I would end the season 12 and 10 with 215 strikeouts. I'd be named the Tourists's Player of the Year and would hold the Rockies's single-season strikeout record for the next thirteen years. My name appeared on the Colorado Rockies scoreboard during an actual game letting the fans know I had thrown a no-hitter. Destiny was in the making and life was about to unfold exactly the way I had planned it.

This wasn't just about one night or one game—this was confirmation! I was on the path to much greater things. This night was not the end of a season, it was the beginning of a career that would define me. This was proof my path was forged in the clay and grass of America's greatest pastime. *I am a professional baseball player.*

It was now 2005, and I'd pitched my last game of the season, again. Seven years prior, I had just thrown my first no-hitter; now I found myself playing for the Bridgeport Bluefish, an independent team in a non-affiliated league. This was not where I, or any other aspiring Major League Pitcher wants to be. I'd just finished my worst season, 4–9 with a 6.89 era. In seven seasons of playing, my future had somehow slipped right through my fingers.

I was supposed to be pitching in the big leagues. I should have already been an all-star. I should have already signed a multi-million dollar contract and won a World Series. My career in baseball was about to see its last inning.

STRIKE THREE

After four surgeries, my arm was trashed, broken and weak. More importantly, so was I. Emotionally drained by the weight of the decision I would soon make, I was letting the voices in my head win the battle. Reconciling failure with one's self is the single hardest thing we can do. It attacks our ego, social reputation, integrity as a person, everything.

My whole life had been dedicated to achieving one goal, one accomplishment, one destiny. How could I go back home, face my family, face my friends, face all those people rooting for and against me? For years, baseball was who I was, and the basis for my "self-worth," and with one final pitch, it would be stripped away.

I convinced my manager, Chico Lind, to let me go home before the season was officially over. I still remember giving him a bottle of Grand Marnier to bribe and thank him for letting me leave. Then, I just walked away and barely said goodbye to my teammates. As I loaded my bags into the car for the trip home, I was learning a new game, one of shame and blame that would last many innings.

Strike three. The game, *my* game, was officially over.

CHAPTER 1

Greatness Escaped

Chasing, wanting, sacrificing, even *living* for something, does not mean it will be. It doesn't guarantee success, even though that's what everyone tells us, teachers, coaches, parents, friends, everyone! Life has no guarantees; we have to create the life we want. There is no manufacturing plant that bottles up success and sells it to you, although they'll try; life is unique to you.

I never had *the* conversation, with myself or anyone else, of what life would look like outside of baseball. Having hard conversations with one's self or with others is not something we seek. Why would we? It's uncomfortable and nobody likes to be uncomfortable. If you avoid this, however, it will wreck you. One day, it *will* happen. The door will close and the jersey will come off.

We never lie in bed, stare at the ceiling and say, "Well if they release me today, that's cool. I'll just do something else." That NEVER happens! People can't just turn off their life's passion and "do something else." I was forced to because my jersey *did* come off. No matter what I tried I couldn't get to the level I aspired to. Read that last line again; that might be the single hardest line I've written in this entire book. It still hurts, but if you let it, pain or the awareness of *past* pain, can be a healthy, even motivating fuel. Our pain can become our testimony.

Now when I look in the mirror and see my shoulder (the crucial tool that was supposed to bring me the completion of my life's work) . . . other than the scars from past surgeries, it looks just like the other shoulder. It's not weak. *We're* not weak. In fact, those who face adversity are far more likely to succeed than those who have the red carpet spread out before them. Adversity is life's weighted vest; it gives us something to carry during the hard times. But it's our choice to carry it, get stronger from it, and at the end of the day, we can take off the vest and enjoy the strength and fitness that comes from making the decision to endure through the struggle.

For countless reasons, thousands of athletes, every year, leave their team or sport and are forced to pack up their dreams along with their personal belongings. They then head back to the life they thought they were never going back to. This hard truth extends to more than just athletes. Musicians, military men and women, mothers, fathers, kids, all kinds of people are faced with unexpected life-changing realities—affecting them both emotionally and mentally. It can be crippling.

If you had told me that I was going to write a book about the rise and fall of my career, I would've laughed and put on my glove as I headed out of the dugout. As I sit here and type this, I am forced to reckon with even that attitude of certainty. Nothing is certain. Writing a book about my rise and fall wasn't in the cards. As you turn these pages and examine the mortal wound of my dreams, I know I'm not alone and neither are you. We all must become warriors of our own light. Light doesn't discriminate—it shines wherever it can.

In the darkest chasms of my being, I knew I needed to write this book. But I hesitated. I thought, *who wants to hear from an old, retired, ex-minor league guy?* I didn't even make it to the big leagues; there really wasn't anything worth writing about. I was just another guy with huge aspirations, even huge potential, but at the end of the day, didn't accomplish what I set out to do. And to be honest, I didn't want to talk (let alone write) about the pain from my past failures knowing it might hurt the people closest to me and bring out those past wounds.

Many of you who are reading this already understand what I'm saying. For years, you have been hiding this pain, letting it seed itself into everything you do. You've been masking your emotions. You've spent years burying the fallout—keeping it out of sight—not just from other people, but even yourself. Yet it persists, manifesting itself in countless ways in your life. This is no way to live; you weren't made for this. Fear of hurting others while we sit in pain is also not fair. I'm not condoning you cutting ties with everyone who's close to you, but you have to understand that people will show friction when you start to grow and change. This is part of the journey. You don't owe them your unhappiness so they can continue on a path you're trying to outgrow.

Perhaps you have tried to communicate your troubling emotions. You open up, feeling vulnerable, experiencing guilt and shame for feeling this way, for not being able to just move on and accept life with a glass half-full. But the people around you just don't get it. *How can you be so lost, unable to adapt, unhappy with your current existence?* Some take it personally, or even feel resentment toward you when you try to talk about it. Their inability to connect with and understand what you're trying to say just furthers the cycle. So you shut it off and ignore it. Those you care about grow more distant. We blanket those changes with our own catch phrases, "everything happens for reason" or "life happens." That's true, life does happen and there is a reason, but neither of these excuses are valid enough to live a life fraught with unfinished business or open wounds.

Forever Chasing

We look back at what once was while being faced with so many uncertainties about the future. We cling to the moments of fulfillment that made us feel good. This is nostalgia distilled. All this does is set up a dichotomy of the search-fulfill cycle. It's addiction at its core and addiction of any kind is weakness. *Which road should I take now? Is this the course I should stay on? Will I ever see that mountain-top again?* (Or like me) *Will I ever reach it for the first time?* I'm not saying you can't remember the good times, but be cautious about the weight you give them, or they will sink you.

My future was mapped out years in advance just like I wanted it. I had an internal vision board before I even knew what a vision board was. A Hall of Fame career, then on to a cherished retirement, living in San Diego, coaching my kids, and playing golf. That was it. I was a pitcher; my skills brought me the life I wanted.

I would often look back on my last season of baseball and question whether I gave up too soon. Was it really supposed to be over? Or did I just cut it short? Walking away from my dream career would start a recurring theme in my life. From then on, there would be many times in my life when I would simply walk away from things I had started.

For years after I left the game, I would cling to the hope of a spring training invite. I could smell the grass and feel my cleats slipping on and picture my hands lacing them up. The feel of the leather glove around my hand was palpable. Often, I would sit at home, holding a baseball as I pictured the sequence of pitches I would prepare to throw that inning.

My dreams felt so real—I desperately wanted them to be. This all sounds very clichéd but you need to hear this from me: it's more than a cliché because it's true. And it sucked! How are we supposed to just carry on when the defining direction in our life is swept away. And in truth, it comes across as not even that big of a deal to the rest of the world: "Oh dang, that kid didn't turn out to be a professional baseball player, oh well." But what that judgment fails to recognize is that it was so much more than that. It was me listening to those around me who said, "You can be anything you want to be if you put your mind to it." Yeah, well I put my mind to it, and my body and my heart and my soul. I did every f%&$ing thing they said I should, and it still didn't work. So no, it's not just "oh dang." It was my life's work punched in the face. The other aspect this judgment fails to consider is that other people hit walls too, not just aspiring professional athletes. Everyday thousands of people get their world turned upside down. Circumstances force people to shift their lives. Re-evaluate their purpose, question their meaning.

About the time I turned 30 is when I realized it was really over—I might as well have been turning sixty. I know I should have gotten the hint much sooner, but I am being completely honest with you. Turning 30 was a horrible experience for me emotionally—the official end of a life chapter, a career, a goal. It was over. It was in the past, and nothing I could do would ever change it. Part of me died that day, but I never buried *him*. That figment of a man would follow me around and haunt me for the coming years. You can't outrun a shadow, but you *can* turn off the light.

Failure sucks—and anyone who downplays it or tells you otherwise is full of crap. The high level of intensity it takes to chase a massive dream or challenge—a destiny waiting to be fulfilled—is beyond the scope for some, and we can't fault them for that, but we need to be aware that each perspective and path is different. When people don't give the same weight to something like failure as you do, it isn't because they haven't failed or have had an easy life (even though we may think that), rather it's because they haven't failed like *we* failed. Not better or worse, just different. However, there is a gap between those who are chasing a dream and those who appear to lack any motivation or vision for what they want, which in and of itself, is its own perilous journey, and we can be glad we aren't on that path.

I've already mentioned that some people think this sounds like no big deal or that I'm pathetic for giving it this much weight in my life. But those people don't understand what it's like to stand in our shoes, the shoes of an athlete who didn't make it as far as they thought they would. I *had* a path I was supposed to walk, and *now*, I never would. The loss of my dream meant my purpose in life was also gone. Deeply ashamed of my failures, I carried heavy guilt that continually slowed me down, leaving me with a life of complacency.

With all these unresolved issues and regrets weighing on me, also stacked on my shoulders was a burden even more troubling—I had lost my identity. Losing one's identity for whatever reason can be a downward spiral. When the completion of the goal becomes the thing we let define us, we sacrifice the ability to be great in anything we do. From that point forward, unless we allow ourselves the grace to grow out of failure, we lose.

My Outside Didn't Match My Insides

Your dreams were too big anyway. That was my new internal dialogue, that was my self-talk. Convincing myself I was average, or even less than average, was how it played out; not just in the endeavor of playing professional baseball, but a *lifetime* failure. I was broken inside, thus unable to begin to relate to what other people were saying about me. Friends and family would tell me, "You were successful. Why can't you see that? You didn't fail. You accomplished more than many of us will ever do."

These comments are hard to hear. I *did* fail based on what I set out to do. And who are they to tell me I succeeded? When people are telling us what we *don't* want to hear, the words are somehow sharper and cut deeper. Remember these are the same people who told me, "You can do anything you put your mind to as long as you work hard . . . " I listened to them with my entire being back then, but now I refused to listen. This is one of the hardest pieces to navigate through. The consistency of others never changes, but our expectations of their interactions with us change based on our own internal successes and struggles.

Now, consider the apologies I had to declare when all this came to a head and I realized what an a-hole I'd been. The people I loved the most, who were closest to me, took the hardest punches in a boxing match that was all my own to fight.

STRIKE THREE

I knew the people giving this encouragement couldn't comprehend the degree of accomplishment I had been seeking—there was a *massive* difference in the magnitude of success they saw in me and what I saw in myself.

My view of myself as a failure diminished many areas in my life, even as I made (albeit failed) attempts to move on. Many people I talk to experience the same thing—bringing no passion to their jobs, relationships, or goals. Even if they have a drive to be successful (and many do), when they achieve their goals, they are still unfulfilled. Such successes just intensify their sense of an inner void.

My fear for so long was that I would always be broken. I would never become the person I was supposed to become. I just told you I would never become who I thought I was supposed to become. This is another one of those hard lines to type. Whether you have heard this or not, I'll say it now: You're not alone in this struggle. This pain is too common and felt by too many of us.

We live in this darkness between an incomplete dream and our potential. One thing we need to change is our perspective of the *entire* scenario. That single act is crucial, and no small undertaking. It must be intentional beyond anything you've ever tried to do. You may think, *how does he know what I tried to do?* Well, because I tried, to.

I would often ask myself, *Why is it the person in the mirror hasn't changed, but the world I live in has?*

We all fabricate ways to numb ourselves when we live a life that's unfulfilled. One of the most blistering experiences we face daily is comparing how people treated us *then* to how they treat us *now*. This is our ego seeking to dominate, and we can't let it. This is unhealthy pride taking over.

Two months after I walked away from baseball, the memory was still a festering wound of pain and depression. With no direction, no education, and too proud to ask for help, I became a real estate agent in Denver, Colorado. It seemed like a decent gig; I could make money, save some face, and ride on the glory story of having played high-level baseball.

One day, I was walking through a neighborhood I identified as a potential farming area. After I knocked on the door of a house nearby, a lady answered and looked at me like I was the door-to-door book salesman from *Office Space*. At that moment, with her staring at me, wearing that contorted look on her face, humility and embarrassment overwhelmed my emotions. Just imagine, two months prior, the same people whose doors I was knocking on for business had been waiting in line for my autograph, a smile, or a picture for their children. I was left with self-pity, insecurity, and emptiness. It was the painful awareness that I was not doing what I wanted to be doing and was bumping through life with no direction.

Many of us knew early who we wanted to become. So we devoted everything to achieve it. We were laser-focused and constantly moving in the direction we envisioned for our lives. For me, it was baseball. Whatever it was for you, it was who *you* were. It was how we were defined, a part of our makeup. We slept it, trained for it, chased it; we loved and hated it (respectfully); it was us, and we were it. For us, there was no Plan B. Plan B only takes energy from Plan A.

We'd spent the better part of our lives doing more than just chasing our dreams. We became obsessed. Ten thousand hours is laughable considering how much more time we actually put in. This pursuit became our significant other. We were married to it, devoted, obsessed, crazy in love with it! It was the unhealthy relationship everyone can see from the outside, but those deep in the middle can't see at all, or don't want to. People on the outside looking in see us as deranged. They just couldn't fathom this level of passion. We were weird to them, but we didn't care. Their opinions didn't matter—we didn't have time to give them a second thought. Until it was over.

Then a shift occurs and their opinions matter all too much. Now that it's all over, we allow their judgments to take ownership in our lives, and we hold them to be true. It's like suddenly we can only pay attention to the trash talk and perceptions that people cast. It is during these times we realize how fragile we are, how much weight we give our ego, but there is an opportunity to take a step back and realize what we truly are about. That's a hard step to take; nobody likes to take a step back, especially athletes. We're bred to charge ahead, take the risk others won't take, and looking back isn't in our DNA.

Instead of defining who *we* are, we let a sport, position or role define us. We allow it to hold us to a specific image, and we lose ourselves in that image. It took me thirteen years to shed the image of myself as a *failed* former professional athlete, rather than as a former professional athlete. That was the hardest 13 years of my life. Most people in their 20s have the fondest memories, and I do too, but I also hated that time when I defined myself as a failure. To this day, it's still there to some extent, and it will never go away. However, now I let that piece of me occupy the appropriate amount of space and hold the appropriate amount of weight.

It merely falls in with the rest of my being like a piece in a puzzle; it is no longer *the* piece. I eventually realized I didn't need it to define me, and neither do you. It's time to rewrite that chapter in your life—from the moment that *defined* you to the moment that will now *refine* you! Each person who is reading this has "that" story, and on the other side of that story, a new one is waiting to be written. The best part is that you get to be the author this time, you choose the setting, scenery, and main character. The sport or position no longer has the lead role. You do. Enjoy this opportunity.

What's Your New Superpower?

Here's an uncommon truth that we not only ignore during those years of chasing the dream, but we deny to be true in our minds completely: We weren't born into this world with just one gift. But, because we realized one gift particularly early in our lives, we focused on it and developed it. We gave little attention to our *other* unique qualities. Our job now is to look into the other areas of ourselves and unearth those skills. They're not new, they've just been buried beneath the dominance of our former self.

It doesn't matter how young or how old you are. Whatever excuses you want to throw out there, they don't matter. In this case, you're not unique. We've said them all to ourselves: *I have no education; I'm a stupid, (old) jock; I'm starting too late in life; If I only*. I've said it, and so have you. Enough of the excuses! For years, we rose to the top of our game. We faced challenges and beat the odds, time and time again. We pushed ourselves more than anyone else could imagine.

Why did you do this? Because you believed in yourself, and you believed in what you were doing. That was why you were created, right? It was your unique talent, and when you did it, every emotion inside you came alive.

Why should now be any different? Those moments can be found again. I'm doing it, and so can you. I say "doing" because you need to know that I'm still very much on this journey. WE are learning together on this; as much as you need someone in your life to help, so do I.

I know you'd like me to tell you that I woke up one day, realized that I needed to change, and I did it. But that simply isn't the case. I knew I had a problem, and I've been working on myself for the past 13 years to fix it. Here I am—a constant work in progress. I still slip into that old space like the way an alcoholic walks by a liquor store and feels that twinge of attraction to go inside.

For too many years in my life, I felt alone on an island. I didn't know the next steps. I didn't know that others felt lost like I did. I made the decision to walk away from the game, and like that, my support system of other like-minded people was gone. The group I had identified with and gone through life with suddenly disappeared. I was an outsider looking in—no longer able to cross over the white chalk lines, enter the locker room, or stand on the top of the mound. I was now a has-been, a statistic. I was no longer a professional athlete. I was now broken and alone.

Every day, people like you and me are left to pick up the pieces of shattered dreams, massive failures, incomplete goals with haunting thoughts of an unfulfilled life. It doesn't have to be this way, hell it *shouldn't* be this. You don't have to search for answers by yourself!

I've come to understand that my purpose and future are far greater than my past failures. Yours can be, too. You have everything it takes to live a life of fulfillment and accomplishment. Begin your journey and start the next chapter of your life. Because the world needs who you want to be, now more than ever.

CHAPTER 2

The Chase

When was the last time you felt alive—on fire for life? Can you remember what that was like? It's locked within the memories from your past. I bet, given close attention, you could almost relive the smells, the sounds, the feelings—the intense emotion of the moments. Having memories like this is a crucial part in making the future we ache for. Our memories are our governing body, self actualized and tailored perfectly to us.

Combing through the things which I took pure joy in, the games I played as a kid and into my professional career, I'm made aware of how instinctively competitive I was. Sports and competition were magnetic for me. I remember the first big red bat my father bought me. It stood 24" tall, and I was only 45" at the time; the barrel was thicker than my thighs. When I gripped it for the first time, I remember thinking how strong I felt swinging it. I could hit the plastic baseballs my father threw me out of any imaginary park.

Growing up, it wasn't just baseball I fell in love with. I loved every sport—football, basketball, wrestling, volleyball, soccer, tennis—anything that involved competition, I was game. I distinctly remember how painful it was not to play basketball as a fourth grader. I remember sitting on the bench watching the "older" kids play. This wasn't fair! During recess, I would be out there schooling them in the same game that, after school, I wasn't invited to play simply because I wasn't old enough. Not because I wasn't good enough, the rules wouldn't allow for it. So I sat impatiently waiting for my turn.

Oftentimes, we wait when in reality, we must *take* it. *You* must decide when it's your turn because nobody else is going to do it for you. There is always going to be an excuse, that you're too tall, short, young, old, etc. The reality is that none of those things matter when it comes to growing yourself.

One year, my father gave me a weighty choice.

"Joshua," he said, "you can either play soccer and T-ball, or move up a level and play single A baseball."

In life we are plagued with "what if" and are often faced with the challenge of "going for it" or not. When your jersey comes off, the feeling is the same. The "what ifs" come back, and now you have to figure out what you should "go for" next.

The thought of giving up two sports was a hard decision, but to play at a higher level against better competition was something I desired even more. This was the first of countless sacrifices I would make to go after something I wanted. I am not sure if at that moment I was cognizant of it or not, but choosing to play single A ball may have been the catalyst for my entire life, and I was only eight!

How can we hinge our entire future on a pattern of sacrifice and passion from a series of decisions we made as children? Easy. Kids do things 100 percent authentically and chase the things that give them pure joy. I was a kid; I liked baseball. Baseball gave me joy. So I played baseball. That slow growth of a skill and cultivation of habitual competition brings us to the point of no return. That journey is a fine one, full of passion, excitement, and obsession!

Growing up in Casper, Wyoming, allowed me to be a big fish in a small pond. Playing on teams with older kids only fueled my passion to compete. Afterward, I had no interest in playing with kids my own age.

No doubt, I competed with a chip on my shoulder, as well. And while this propelled me past my opponents, it effectively isolated me from my own peers. Another sacrifice I would make to face better competition. At this point, however, I couldn't grasp the implications of these decisions.

I was taught to be confident, stand up for myself, and to work hard. These are the things kids should be taught, but for the better part of my youth, my confidence would often be seen as arrogance. Regretfully, that interpretation was generally well deserved. Admittedly, I was arrogant. There are many hard conversations woven into these pages that I have had to have first with myself before they could make it into this book. Arrogance was one of those hard conversations.

Because of my relentless pursuit to win at all costs, I was not the team player who embodied camaraderie, nor did I know how to deal with losing. Of all the things I regret in my career (and sports life in general), not being a great teammate is definitely at the top of my list. Today, as I coach my children and their teams, I work to instill some simple truths regarding teamwork and what it takes to be a good teammate. Traits I wish I had embodied more of when I played. You might wonder how a guy who was never a good teammate can coach little kids to be good teammates, but a person who's always been thirsty can appreciate a glass of water far more than a person who knows no thirst. I knew what being a good teammate looked like, I had some of the best. I just didn't give it the attention it deserved.

Trust Your Team

The eight traits that every player should embody:

Give credit to the entire team for the win.
Show your team they can trust you.
Take responsibility when bad things happen.
Be present in the moment.
Be a student first.

Celebrate your wins.
Don't take it so personally,
and always, always be willing to improve.

These may seem like standard skills and tools everyone has in their arsenal, but I didn't. They were never fully developed in me, and I am willing to bet that they weren't fully instilled in you either. Don't take this as me blaming coaches or mentors; I've taken complete responsibility. I just didn't value them as much as I should have. Winning and making it known that I was good enough to win mattered more than "being present in the moment." I always had my eyes centered on what was to come. It took years for me to uncover and live out these skills. My baseball career had come and gone well before I began to develop them for myself. When I did, they became the foundation for my growth as a man.

We all have a foundation, good, bad, or otherwise. I had some of the best parents anyone could hope for, and great coaches too, but I *still* lost my way. Remember in chapter one, I talked about those people who told me I could do anything I wanted, and I listened. Then they told me I wasn't a failure, and I didn't listen. The thing with parents and coaches is, they try to see the best in you, and thank God for that!

Let me expand on the common metaphor of having a solid foundation. When building a house, you must first pour a foundation; however, in order for the foundation to be solid, it must have rebar in it. Rebar is the reinforced steel that gives concrete unified strength and integrity. Cracks will happen, but with the rebar in place the foundation will not crumble. This ties into the idea that we all have a foundation, but some of us may not have the much needed rebar to solidify our foundation. It's up to you to cut out the broken chunks of your foundation and install the much needed strength. Yes, it's a lot of work, and no one can do it for you.

Rebar

In life we must always be examining the things that hold us together. We must view very closely the things that break us apart. Rebar in your life can be the simple things such as your circle of influence, your board table, your goals, routines, the daily disciplines you deploy to keep growing. We all know the feeling of losing ourselves suddenly and how hard it is to get back to center. However, the idea of rebar in our lives goes much deeper: it is our moral compass, integrity, fortitude, courage, endurance, wisdom, faithfulness to name a few. Rebar is the discipline and grit we need in order to become our best self. It gives us the strength to make the right decisions. It shows up when we handle the temptations we are confronted with. From making quick purchases to big life decisions. It all needs to be looked at regularly, tested and reinforced. We must make sure we don't neglect what holds us together. As you're faced with new challenges, always check the rebar.

Remember the sharply focused dream you chased. Recall how it felt when you were living out your deepest passion or what you may have even considered your purpose. For a little while (or your entire life), perhaps like me, you were willing to sacrifice everything it was going to take to accomplish this dream you had.

I wasn't joking when I mentioned earlier how having this type of passion in our lives can be like a significant other. Have you ever pushed yourself further than you thought possible? Did you ever sacrifice nights out with people, parties with friends, personal relationships—memories never to be experienced because the goal you were chasing was the only thing on your mind?

I chased greatness.

I bled for greatness.

I challenged and pushed myself to the extremes for greatness.

I clawed my way up to try and achieve something very few people would ever dream about pursuing. And yet, it still wasn't enough. At a certain point though, the talent pool gets so lean and mean that even I started to question if I could keep up. So I worked even harder and did what they told me. Maybe my body gave out, maybe my talent wasn't deep enough, or maybe time slipped away. Whatever the reason, it came to pass that my massive dream eluded me, and the experience left me broken and wounded.

No matter what people say, it brings no solace because we were once on a mission, and *it felt so good to be on that mission.*

The Notion We All Have Greatness within Is a Lie

We were created *by* greatness. Because of this, we were created with uniqueness. And as a result, it is our job to discover our uniqueness and *make it our greatness.*

The idea of having greatness in us is a paralyzing thought. Ask yourself and be honest: What are you great at? Ninety-nine percent of you won't be able to answer with anything. Most of the time, this assumption of greatness is based on a comparison to others, which really does nothing for us but bolster our insecurities because we always adjust our comparison for a losing outcome. If you have an answer, you are either a complete egomaniac or maybe—just maybe—you've already discovered your uniqueness and honed it to the point where you truly have turned it into your greatness.

You must understand we all have unique qualities, which—if focused on, practiced, and lived out—can be turned into greatness in our lives. Athletics was my uniqueness and baseball became the way I displayed my greatness to the world. It defined and consumed me.

It was my 18th birthday, and all the work I had done from that moment when I decided to move up to A ball was starting to pay off. All the naysayers who thought I wasn't good enough, or paid lip service to me and smiled when I told them I wanted to be in the major leagues were starting to think I might actually get there. My senior year of high school was in full swing. I was training hard both in and outside of school. I guess I was just like every other high school kid in some ways. In other ways I was totally different.

I didn't party much and wasn't consumed with what everyone else was doing. All I cared about was sports and whichever girl I was dating at the time. That's it.

Then a phone call came. A call that changed my life forever and reinforced the hard work I had done for the previous ten years. I had been drafted by the Colorado Rockies! A dream come true. This achievement felt surreal, yet it wasn't unexpected. Read that again! I had wholly expected it to happen; my faith in myself was so strong I knew getting drafted was everything but inevitable. This wasn't about luck or chance; this was simply about my destiny, something I had worked so hard for. When we are consumed by our goals, it's easy to explain why something worked or why it didn't; we can (and are taught to) make adjustments if needed. I believed all along that what I was doing would result in the perfect scenario. Being drafted by a major league baseball team. And it did, **BOOM** I win! See that confidence borderline arrogance right there? It all seems normal when you're on the inside looking out.

Statistics show out of 440,000 high school baseball players, 200 will make it to the majors. That's 1 out of the best 2,200 high school baseball players! I had a 0.00045 percent chance of making it. But here's the thing, I was certain I would be one of the 200 kids who would. People buy lottery tickets every day. This wasn't just a lottery ticket. This was thousands of hours realized. This *was* my destiny.

I'm going to lay out a concept here that we will work with from this point forward. We are all born into this world with different genetic makeup, and as we grow, we have different experiences, and we are all divinely unique. So if we are all unique, either because of our life's experiences or because God made us that way (or both), then as we grow and hone our paths, passion, and direction, we are living out that uniqueness. This is not where *this* book turns into *that* book and tells you you're all unique and special. It is however, undeniable that each and every one of us walks a different path in this world, and by default, that makes us ALL one of a kind.

Everyone's perspective is different because everyone has lived a different life. Let's position this unique journey as a crucial part of your being. You must grow and cultivate that unique set of experiences into something greater. I didn't realize it when I was 8, or 18, but that is what I was doing. My mistake came when I failed to see the value in this ever-changing absolute. The fact that my unique take on this thing we call "life" is still unbelievable without baseball, and it was still going to grow and change even when I left the mound. I just never knew how much growth and change I could personally influence in my life.

When you are working toward and living out your uniqueness, it should make *you* (and those around you) *feel fulfilled*. We live in a world replete with false narratives of what being fulfilled looks like. Today, it's all about us as individuals. "You do you" they say. We're so focused on how others "should" make us feel, instead of giving attention to what we ourselves are contributing. We often miss the point that when we do experience fulfillment, it comes from how we impact other people.

As parents we tend to leverage sports as a way to raise our kids. It's marketed that way, and the statistics back it. If a kid is in sports, he is more likely to graduate high school, less likely to get into trouble after school, more likely to develop teamwork skills, less likely to be selfish, etc. Sports are a great social outlet for kids. It is during these young years of extracurriculars where grit is cultivated and confidence is gained (or lost). It's where we learn what it feels like to be part of something. That's all very much the goal and drive of what we, along with our parents and coaches are doing when we play sports as young kids. Unfortunately, it's not all good though.

Sports can also warp us into becoming a person who cares only about success. I mentioned "being a part of something" earlier. If done wrong,

STRIKE THREE

it will lead to an unhealthy desire for acceptance, where confidence becomes arrogance, grit becomes the need to win above moral and ethical behavior, and the common goal becomes your goal alone. It's all a matter of how you look at it and the precedence you set for yourself during these times.

And what a task it can be to navigate all these dynamics as an adolescent. It's tremendously difficult. I know, I lived it. I mentioned earlier that my confidence was often taken as arrogance and those were probably accurate judgments. But I need to bring that back up now as it was a blanket covering huge insecurities—including the uncomfortable notion that we, as a family, didn't fit in. I was the oldest of 6, which meant I was also the "babysitter," much to my embarrassment. And because of this and many other decisions that my parents made, we didn't have money for nice things and we often went without; at least, that was the story I was telling myself.

My dad was a carpenter, not a lawyer, surgeon, dentist, nor did he have a job rich, successful men have. Growing up, we were always the kids in the cargo van showing up to baseball practice. People stared at us. I didn't know the narratives they were spewing into their friends' ears at the time; I just knew it didn't feel good and I was embarrassed. That dynamic fueled the unhealthy side of my drive. On the field or court, it didn't matter how many kids were in our big Catholic family, or what my dad did for work. What mattered was how hard I worked at practice and that I was more skilled than those around me.

Sports brought out the confidence in me that I had been longing for in my life. Sports gave me the opportunity to prove I was worth something. Again, this sounds typical but I had that inferiority complex that everyone talks about. I hated the fact that the other kids and parents put out that "they-don't-belong" vibe to us. I lived in scarcity for many years in my youth. Never having enough. Always being told we couldn't afford it. Always going without.

It's taken two decades to shed that perception of not belonging, living with scarcity in my life. It's been a really difficult journey. It came at the expense of those around me. Much like the countless little sacrifices I made to get to the professional level in baseball, so did the slow unraveling of this mindset and the cultivation of a new perspective. The perspective that I could actually take joy and find satisfaction in helping others be great. This very complicated truth allowed me to pour some of that confidence into the lives of others.

When we live out the qualities of selflessness and self-awareness in our lives, we begin taking ownership of living life differently by living it authentically. We start to realize what it truly takes to be the person we've been searching for all our lives, to be the person we absolutely love being.

When we are not being true to ourselves, we live life in scarcity and regret. We create a life that is never what we want, but what we think we should want. This puts us in a cycle where we seek fulfilment, then move onto the next thing and do the same; it's very shortsighted and lacks the depth we need to truly be fulfilled. We cut short our potential and believe that others who have become successful are somehow stealing our joy and success.

Integrity Moments

So, what do you do? How do you right the ship, change course, and correct the direction of your life? *Integrity*. Now here is a word so overused it can lose its impact and become easy to pass by. It makes an appearance in every mission statement you come across, every creed a company shares. It's in value propositions galore, and when people rant to others, it is usually one of the qualities they claim for themselves, but say other people lack.

However, just because this word is overused and underappreciated doesn't mean it is not a powerful, honorable word that should still be

STRIKE THREE

a staple in your life. Understand though, there is a difference between living *with* integrity and living *in* integrity. Too many people live *with* integrity in their lives. They believe they can take it with them, but then sometimes leave it in the other room while they make decisions based on their emotions or their justifications. Too many times we hear of a professional athlete, a government official, a CEO of a company making completely irrational decisions in the moment that end up ruining their careers.

Beginning to live *in* integrity is the shift we need. Then, we never leave integrity anywhere, and it never leaves us. When we leave a room, it is still in us. When we go behind closed doors, it's there too. A great friend of mine told me, "People judge themselves by their intentions, but they will judge you by your actions." That's a hard thing for us all to admit and correct in our own lives. You must make a commitment and say, "No more!" You must scream it, declare it, and own it. You must create integrity moments within yourself by deciding to live *in* integrity. It is not a question of whether you can, but a question of how badly you want to. Start making integrity moments in your life, and you'll be amazed to see how much your life changes. The moment you begin to judge others by their intentions and yourself by your actions, is the moment you start living *in* integrity!

If you had what it took to get as far as you did in your chosen sport or field, you have everything it takes inside you to make that decision today to live differently. You may not believe, as I didn't; just start small. Like T-ball small, like lower-the-hoop-small. It's the little things you do every day that reinforce the bigger direction in your life. Stop hitting the snooze button, do a morning walk or meditation session, learn what it means to "fill your cup." This isn't some massive shift you can make all at once in your life; it's a series of small choices you need to begin making. Because at the end of the day, too many things are completely out of our control.

Too Good to Be True

This was the day you never want to experience. My shoulder was popping again (we'll talk about injuries later), exactly like it did when it had torn before. Everything inside me said it was broken, but I kept holding out hope. As the months inched closer to spring training, my shoulder was not progressing, and in April 2001, I would go in for yet another surgery. This time, my shoulder would have to be immobile for thirty days, which led to, you guessed it, another problem—a frozen shoulder.

This is called *adhesive capsulitis*. Where after a surgery the immobilization results in scar tissue bearing down on the shoulder's range of motion and ability to move. During therapy, my shoulder would be manipulated in order to free the scar tissue, allowing me to regain my throwing motion. For the next couple of months in rehab, I was beyond thrilled—the surgery was working! Though I was still a work in progress, I could just tell my shoulder was healing. *Man this feels good,* I would often say to myself.

If you've never experienced a torn shoulder, understand that it's impossible to sleep on, let alone perform as an athlete. The burning becomes unbearable. Prior to my surgeries and every day thereafter, I did whatever I could do to get my shoulder prepared for the next day, the next game, the next season. In order to take away the pain and prepare for the next game, I would ingest as many anti-inflammatories as needed. Depending on their strength, that could be as much as a heavy dose of five at a time, a couple of times a day. It was only temporary, after all. The pain couldn't last my entire career, right? My liver and kidneys could handle it; heck, I was a professional athlete, right?

I was sitting in my rehab chair when my physical therapist put my shoulder in the usual position. He would lift my elbow up to the side as he was pressing down on my shoulder. He started to manipulate it, and then . . . POP! The labrum had torn yet again. This was a puke-inducing

STRIKE THREE

sound. Aside from the pain and flood of emotions, the pure sound was gut-wrenching.

My mind immediately focused me in another direction. Away from the reality of the situation. I started thinking about what it meant for me to sign with the Rockies. It was like being drafted by the New York Yankees. As a kid from Wyoming, Colorado was practically my home state. The ink was still drying on the contract, and I recall this sensation of a great weight being lifted off my shoulders (well, one of them anyway). From the time of my earliest memories, I'd carried two chips on those shoulders: proving people wrong about me, and proving my father right. He never doubted I could play professional baseball. As the oldest of 6 siblings, I resented the responsibility that went along with being the oldest. I hated being constantly told we couldn't afford anything. I hated that we were just different, and that my folks actually took pride in that. When I signed that contract, all of that resentment, anger, and jealousy went away.

That was a defining moment in my life. All the self-doubt and insecurities simply vanished, temporarily. I saw my family in a different light. I saw my responsibility as a brother in a whole, new way. I now saw myself as the one who would change my family's destiny. It's both bold and tragic. The culmination of my life's work, completed at the age of 20, was materialized in a signature on a line. Again, that arrogance I've referred to before plays out here. Who was I to change my family's destiny by becoming a professional baseball player? I mean really, was I that shallow to think that my humble blue collar dad who worked his ass off for his entire family could be defined by his oldest son's signing with the Rockies? Though the actions were misguided the intentions were noble. It wasn't about overshadowing my father but it was about setting my family on a different course. A better course. A "successful" course. My understanding of what success really means in life needed to be rediscovered and God was going to make sure my journey would uncover its deepest meaning.

After my first professional stint in Portland, Oregon, for short-season A-Ball, I went on to fall ball in Phoenix, Arizona, and managed to put together a pretty good season. However, I needed some rest, and the off-season was calling. Over the next two seasons, I would post numbers good enough to be named Colorado Rockies's "Pitcher of the Year" for Asheville, North Carolina. The following year, in Salem, Virginia, I was named to the all-star team and was the Carolina "Pitcher of the Year." I threw a twenty-strikeout game, and later on, a no-hitter. I led the league in ERA (earned run average), strikeouts, and almost led the league with wins, losing out by only a few. I led the Colorado Rockies's entire organization in strikeouts for 13 years. Baseball America rated me as the circuits #10 prospect. My career continued to post highlights, assuring me that the big leagues were merely a few steps away.

As I looked up at the physical therapist I knew exactly what that "pop" meant. Everything had been going so well on my road to recovery, and my trainer later tried to reassure me it was just scar tissue. But I knew better. Not wanting to admit I'd had another failed surgery, I worked diligently to get better. I continued my steady dose of anti-inflammatories and did everything I could possibly do to get myself back to being the pitcher I believed I could still be.

During one of the lowest points in my career, my shoulder felt like it was barely holding on. I was taking too many anti-inflammatories, and at the same time, I had caught a cold. I was miserable. For two days, I didn't leave the hotel room, and hardly even got out of bed.

A short time later, I started feeling better, but I began experiencing heartburn like never before. Anytime I would eat anything or take a drink, it would engulf me. My chest would burn horribly. For the next ten days, my life was a living hell. I drank water only when I was prepared for the heartburn to return. I lost fourteen pounds. I was already skinny enough, and losing any weight wasn't good. Finally, I was admitted to the hospital for fluids and to find out what the heck was going on.

STRIKE THREE

The doctors would later diagnose me with a stomach that had herniated into my esophagus. Whenever I ate or drank, the intensity of the heartburn caused the tissue in my esophagus to burn and turn into ridges, and the diameter of my airway would shrink to one-quarter the size of a normal male throat. Because of my constricted passageway, I would consistently choke on food. To this day, I can't swallow pills, and I have to have my esophagus stretched every couple of years in order for it to remain open enough to swallow food without the fear of choking. I would learn during this time that the massive amounts of anti-inflammatories I was taking had caused my herniated esophagus issue.

The problems caused by this situation continue to plague me still—a reminder of the price I was willing to pay to reach the goal in front of me. How many times have you had someone question if you were willing to pay the price for success? Paying the price doesn't seem that bad while you're doing it—it's the effect on the life you live after your dream ends that you begin to pay interest on the charges made years before.

How many of you are dealing with physical, mental, or spiritual issues because it was part of the price you were willing to pay in order to chase that dream? I may not have the physical scars many athletes bear (I do have a few!); however, like many of us, I have emotional scar tissue that can freeze up my ability to go forward in life. The problem with emotional scars is that they are hidden; we mask them in many different ways. We pick up addictions, we misdirect, and we find ways to numb ourselves to the pain. But they are always there, lurking, even if subdued for a time. No amount of pills or alcohol can reduce the pain of lost emotions.

After the Game Is Over

After the game, I lost who I was.
I lost my identity.
I lost a piece of my soul when the dream died.

Craig Groeschel said, "Our life is the sum total of all the decisions we make, good and bad. Who you are today is a result of all the habits and decisions you make. They all matter, and they all add up over time."

I was twenty-six when my baseball career ended, and the reality of my "failed" life was now starting to sink in. I was truly the sum total of all the good and bad decisions I made in my life. I started to believe that I was being punished for all the bad decisions and choices I made—maybe my baseball career was stripped away from me because of the person I had become, or more importantly, the man I had not.

This would be the beginning of an enormous amount of blame, shame, and guilt that I would carry deep inside me. Because I didn't have the tools to deal with this failure, I masked it. I put on a smile and showed up in life. For the next nine years, I would drift in and out of a living lie. I just put in the time each day to get to the next day.

I was now thirty-five, and I was crying out for transformation in my life. I had recently been to a conference and heard a message about transformation. The speaker, Matthew Kelly, spoke about ". . . going into the deep and closing the chapters in your life that aren't serving you." Serving me? For far too many years, I'd felt caged by my failures, imprisoned by my doubts and shame. Now someone was telling me that I could be transformed, that I could go into the deep and willfully close this chapter of my life and start anew?

I'm sure I had heard similar speeches before, read books that spoke about similar topics, but this was different. This made sense. This resonated with me. I felt it, a subtle pull, a small tug inside me, and I began to ache for something greater. The fire I had felt so long ago started to flicker again. Why this time though? Was it timing, or had I matured enough or become desperate enough to make this time matter more than the others? Could I free myself of this burden? It didn't matter! I needed it now! Maybe you are in this place I found myself. Maybe you need to hear this message too. If so, listen up! You need to decide how bad you want to get on with your life. No one can make that decision for you.

It was hard to believe I could feel more alive and younger at the age of 35; but I did. Not only could I see the possibility, I could feel it. Though I didn't have any answers to my questions yet, I had hope in my life again. I started to believe I could actually live a purpose-filled life. On a much deeper level, maybe I didn't have to settle for average anymore.

Does something inside you ache for more? Do you want to close a long chapter in your life and start a new one? Do you want to start fresh and head into uncharted territory? Do you want to stop being just average?

I believe you can find purpose and meaning in your life, even AFTER the dream is over. And I believe you can live a life of fulfillment AFTER the dream has died. I believe you can live a life on fire with passion, intensity, conviction, and certainty. Why? Because if a has-been, uneducated, broken, old jock can pick himself up after 13 years of doubt, guilt, shame, and uncertainty . . . anybody can. You have a destiny that nobody else can live except you. I don't even know you, but I believe in you, and right now I might be the only one between the two of us who does. Let's change that.

CHAPTER 3

Be the Inspiration You Need

There wasn't a professional baseball team in the country sending scouts to track down a 6'2" 175-lb kid living in Casper, WY. Proximity matters, and it would change my life.

We were scheduled to play the Rapid City Post 22 Legion team on our home field; I didn't know if I was scheduled to pitch in the series, however I found myself on the mound that evening. With no clue of who was in the stands besides my father, I threw a seven-inning shutout with fourteen strikeouts. Come to find out, there were professional scouts watching 2 other players from Post 22, not this skinny, left-handed kid.

Ken Coleman talks about being at the right place at the right time in his book, *The Proximity Principle*. I believe it because I lived it. My career started because of it. That one game set my life on a completely different course. Because the scouts were watching other players they ended up noticing me. Yes, I had a great game. I made an impression. But something far greater happened. I realized I needed to work harder than ever before if I wanted to chase my dream of becoming a professional athlete. So I did. I would experience amazing success and walk through tremendous battles. During this time I would build friendships and destroy relationships. I would do the best I knew how, all while making mistakes, discovering the life I wanted to live, and realizing how far I still needed to go.

Three years out from the time of my release by the Colorado Rockies, I'd had one spring training with the Boston Red Sox and now was playing independent baseball for the Bridgeport Bluefish. My arm was shot, and my spirit was, too.

At the age of 25 my career was spiraling down. With all the chaos and uncertainty going on in my life it's hard to imagine that something good could actually happen. As one chapter was beginning to close another was beginning to open. A different kind of chapter.

Earlier that year, I married *her*. I married *the one*. We dated for nearly a year before I proposed, but I knew within months she would be the person with whom I could easily spend a lifetime. Kate was everything I never knew I needed. If you've ever watched the movie *Doc Hollywood*, with Michael J Fox you'll get it when I say *I married Vialula*. She was down-to-earth, witty, spontaneous, sporty, and could handle herself in any situation! Kate stole my heart within minutes of our first meeting even though I'm certain she didn't know what she had done at the time.

This was supposed to be where life together got better, where my career took off. As a man of faith, I knew for sure God was going to fix my arm and I could do the rest. God didn't fix my arm. I couldn't do the rest. I didn't know it at the time, but my year with the Bridgeport Bluefish would be the last time I would wear a uniform, the last time I would ever stand on the mound as an athlete.

I made my last start. I had thrown my last pitch.

Many of us have the "last time" memory. I still remember the game. What was it for you? Can you remember the last moment? Can you still remember that single instant? That ignition point for the forced direction change in your life? For years, I would bury this part of my life, choosing to avoid the memories, the games, the teammates, the stories. Doing this hurt as bad as my arm did most days. They say time heals all wounds. That's BS! They rot you from the inside. Unless you face the wounds and embrace them, they never go away.

Forgiving the Debt

In her book, *Rising Strong*, Brené Brown says: "Suffering that is not transformed is transmitted to others. . . . There are too many people today who, instead of feeling hurt, are acting out their hurt; instead of acknowledging pain, they're inflicting pain on others. Rather than feeling disappointment, they are choosing to live disappointed."

That was me. Is it you? In your life, right now, are you the person you promised others and yourself to be? 1 Corinthians 13:4, "Love is patient, love is kind, love does not envy." I couldn't get past the first three lines without failing miserably in my life. Never having dealt with my wounds, I couldn't be patient; I was always on edge. I couldn't be kind because everything was always a competition, and I was constantly trying to prove my self-worth. I was tremendously envious of others. They were succeeding, and no matter what I did to win or accomplish something, it was never going to be enough for me.

My entire understanding of my life's purpose was wrong!

When is enough, enough? Have you reached the breaking point? Have you apologized so many times to loved ones that you're running out of excuses for acting the way you do? Are you exhausted from fighting the battles within yourself?

Embrace the pain. Too many of us avoid the pain by ignoring the wound. Now it's time to call it out. You have a catcher hiding behind home plate, but you have to throw the first pitch to start the game. Grab hold of that wound by the stitches and send it. You're not meant to stumble through life. Until you take hold of your life by getting back on the mound, the struggle will always control you. You'll never be able to embrace the new successes in your life because you'll always compare them to the ones you once had.

For far too many years, the pain of my past failure ruled me. It controlled and limited my thoughts; it held me down. But worst of all, it kept me from leading a life I should have been embracing.

Making that switch is only possible if you are able to face this reality. You must forgive yourself for what you're calling a failure.

Until you come face-to-face with the reality that you are worthy of forgiveness, you will continue to allow the negative self-talk to dominate your script. You will always talk yourself into returning to that pit of despair and worthlessness. You must forgive the debt—the debt you believe you owe yourself for the failures in your life. You must open your eyes to the true potential you possess. Step out of your doubts. What can success look like in your life now?

Success in my teens was hitting the home run, throwing the touchdown pass, winning the game. Success in my twenties was signing the contract to play professional baseball, chasing the dream, chasing the lifestyle. Success in my thirties was surviving the financial bust, making our house payment, providing so Kate could stay at home with our children. Now, success looks a lot different: It's about impact, it's about significance, it's about improving the lives of those around me.

We need to find fulfillment. Emptying ourselves into others for their betterment is a true goal we must endeavor toward daily. Would you inspire your past self? If the answer is no, you are in need of change. I can't tell you exactly when you'll see it or realize it, but I do know this: *The fire and the desire you are searching for can be alive in your soul again.*

> *You can spend your life any way you want to but you can only spend it once.*
>
> —John C Maxwell

STRIKE THREE

Move Your Finish Line

You have to move your finish line. At the time I didn't realize that life was not over when the game was over. Nor did I realize that my finish line was actually my starting line. However, it was the journey of self-discovery—the path of MOST resistance—that made the biggest impact. If I were to have skipped out on all the emotions, the disappointments, the heartbreaks, the insecurities, the failures, the challenges, the mistakes, and the pain, I wouldn't be sitting here writing this book. I wouldn't be sharing my struggles. I wouldn't be living this intentional life!

Along the journey to discover myself, it became apparent that in order to do this I needed to know who I wanted to discover. If I could create my best self, what would he look like? So, I started with my personal mission statement. If I was going to reinvent this man, I needed to have a vision of who I needed to become.

Through much prayer and self discovery, came my mission statement: *I will live a life of exceptional impact, influence, and faith. It is my mission to empower people to take ownership of themselves, their families, and those they lead, so they may live a life of exceptional impact, influence, and faith.* It has been my guiding light as I navigate the obstacles, the road blocks, the distractions along the way.

So, who do you want to discover? And when you find that person, what version of yourself is he or she? The best? You should be searching for nothing less.

In 2014, I received the Local Realtor of the Year award for the state of Wyoming. This happened to be the perfect opportunity for leadership growth within the Wyoming Association of Realtors. In spite of this accomplishment, my success felt rather hollow, more like a cover up.

Once again, I was tying my self-worth to personal achievements; it's so hard to break this cycle. And for small moments, I would enjoy the thrill of it. But eventually, like every business venture I started, it would leave me unfulfilled, and therefore, unmotivated. I still hadn't moved my finish line.

My mind had me convinced I was a failure and that my chance for greatness had died the day I left my baseball career behind; something inside me ached for more. Though I could not define it or even put my finger on it, something was always lurking inside me. Since I didn't know what I was looking for, I had no way of connecting with it. My mind distracted me from it, my habits suppressed it, and my emotions kept it buried. I would continue to cycle through this process of gaining some mild awareness, followed by distraction and suppression.

I developed a mask under the guise of being a workaholic. I would use business ventures to feed my ego and build up my sense of self-worth, convincing people I was who I wanted them to see. But my decisions would often be emotional, and not rational. At some level, I was disengaged for all these reasons, and though I longed inside for more, a sense of shame stalked me. Even so, I couldn't let go of the notion that I wanted more authenticity in my life. I knew it was out there somewhere.

Like so many, we seek an external comfort to cover an internal discomfort. I was no different. There are many places in this book where I think, *this is so clichéd; who would read this?* Then I remember, too many people do the same thing; they cover it up with some outside substance or activity, which means we need to address it. This is not a book about overcoming an addiction. This is about overcoming the falsities in your life with real lasting change. It's about taking back the power you gave away!

So, what about this concept of *moving your finish line*? That's the approach you need to take in your life every time a challenge hits you, a dream dies, a failure happens. Every set back or even accomplishment must only help you move your finish line toward a greater goal, a greater accomplishment, a greater vision of your life.

STRIKE THREE

For far too long, I refused to move my finish line, and it kept me looking back on the wrong dream, trapped on a treadmill headed to nowhere. You might be thinking that "moving your finish line" means shortening it, or adjusting it to guarantee success. It's not that at all.

We often view the finish line as the end of the last season we played. We view the finish line as when our dream ended, when we said the words "I'm finished." It's not. When I say we need to move the finish line, what I'm saying is that we need to move it further ahead of ourselves.

Once I moved my finish line, my path became clearer and my destination came into focus. Where do you need to move your finish line and chalk the lines for your next race?

CHAPTER 4

Soul Search

Passion vs. Purpose

We are—original works of art. No two of us alike. Yes, we share similarities as human beings, but there is no other YOU. There is no duplicate. You were divinely *created*, which means your life cannot be an accident. Of course, if that's true, then neither can your failures. Don't pass that last part by too fast. Read it again. If you are not an accident, neither is your life, neither is every failure you've experienced, every decision you've made.

No two of us go through our existence exactly the same, and that *is* freaking AMAZING! It's okay to believe you have something to offer. You need to give yourself this permission. You don't accidentally come to a place in your life where you choose to grow and take ownership. Rooting ourselves in the humble understanding that we *do* have purpose is a crucial ingredient for us to move forward.

I spent years convinced that I was a failure and had created a life I didn't want. I believed for a time I had been given a golden ticket. And through my own faults and poor decisions, blew it. I had created something alright—a world of confusion, loss, despair, and disappointment. And I was the king and owner of it all. Good or bad, our choices define our lives. From the small choices of hitting the snooze button, missing the workout, or arriving to the crucial meeting unprepared, to the big choices of which career path we choose. It's a pretty amazing opportunity quite honestly. When I chose to view everything in my life as happening "for" me and not "to" me, the game changed drastically. It was a small mental shift that resulted in massive changes.

When we confuse our passions with our purpose, we trade in our purpose for our dreams. This is a mistake. Is it really a surprise when we are defeated and crushed when those dreams die? Because, in that scenario, what we think actually died was our purpose in life. Your dreams are just the avenue by which you're choosing to manifest your unique ability and the desires burning in your heart. If everything we are holding onto is wrapped in this essential dream we believe will materialize our purpose in life, is it any wonder so many people experience depression, suicide, substance abuse, toxic relationships, failed marriages, you get my point. This pattern sets us up for failure!

Dream and Search—Repeat

When my baseball career was over, I lived with this constant sense of false urgency in my life. I would wake up in the morning already feeling that I had lost. Already feeling that I had failed. I was supposed to be this confident, secure, focused, decisive man. At the age of 28, I felt like I was already behind the eight ball. My friends had graduated college, been in the work force, and knew the path they wanted to pursue. They were chasing their dreams, and here I was trying to figure out where the hell mine went.

Eventually, I came to realize the reason for my impatience was that I was always searching. Searching restlessly for the next goal, the next accomplishment, the next idea. The truth I discovered was simple yet profound. My life was incomplete because every day I woke up knowing I wasn't the man I *could* be. I needed to adjust my understanding of what it was to be great—by shifting from an intangible dream to a tangible set of actions that would have a result I could see.

STRIKE THREE

When I finally stopped and looked at my life, I realized this urgency came from never achieving the level of success I'd always expected from myself. And as each day passed, I chalked up one more day of failure. I was constantly searching for the future me—the better me, the more accomplished me, *the worthy me*. When I would accomplish something, the joy and celebration were always temporary, always fleeting. The accomplishments themselves were typically materialistic. Temporary satisfaction would follow, but never genuine peace. So, I would continue to dream and search . . . I was comparing every current success against my past failures. Giving more credence to my failures than the wins. If we cover every success we have with the blanket of past failures, how can we expect to feel good about ourselves?

Unfortunately, for many of us, this pursuit of our dreams is what can actually crush us, leading us down a cyclical path of mediocrity and unfulfillment. We get lost in our dreams and in the disappointment of never achieving them. So, we give up . . . on ourselves.

At an early age, we are taught to dream and imagine a life of endless possibilities. It's a shame that as we grow up, we learn to shut down and not share our dreams. We learn how hurtful people can be. Just how ready and willing people are to put us back in place when we demonstrate a desire to reach higher. Don't believe me; when's the last time you told your friends, peers, family, or even your spouse, a crazy, exciting, ridiculously amazing dream of yours? We don't do that, because it's not received with enthusiasm, let alone encouragement. Painful experiences have trained us to keep it in. Instead, we listen to the all-too-familiar voices in our head: *You can't do that! Everyone will laugh at you. Who do you think you are? That's arrogant. Don't be so materialistic.* And not only do we listen to these voices, we take ownership of what they're saying.

What if we didn't. What if we started dreaming more? What if we chose to live a life *on fire*? A fearless life of courage? What if you were to start living your life for YOU? What would this person look like? Who would this person have to be?

Your Purpose

You will never find your purpose without first dedicating time to identify your passion. Passion is simply the emotion we feel that excites us. Passion gives us inner strength to push through, energy to keep going, excitement when things work out. Passion is what we rely on in order to get out of bed earlier, to do that extra rep, to make that extra phone call, to read that extra ten minutes. Passion gives us the strength to go through failure and heartbreak in order to pursue something amazing in our lives. As great as this seems, passion is also an emotion that can be taken away from us. It can be lost, and we've all seen it happen. Many of us have the scars to prove it.

Purpose—our purpose—is something that we don't have control over. At first this sounds like we have no control, but that's not it at all. Purpose is something we discover as we claw our way out of this despair-threaded existence. Purpose brings us to a new understanding of what we are capable of. Read this next sentence very carefully. *We cannot lose our purpose because we did not create our purpose. Our purpose will be with us our entire lives.*

Remember the shadow of failure I mentioned in chapter one, saying we can't outrun it but we could turn off the light? Purpose has its own light, and it has no switch; it's always on. However, it is often buried by our failures when we choose to play the victim. Remember those hard days when you defined your life by the dream you were chasing? Your purpose knows better than to let a dream define you.

Now let's make a distinction: While we didn't *choose* our purpose, we must *choose* to live it. It's called free will. Many people choose not to pursue their purpose because it takes sacrifice, it takes giving up being comfortable, it takes tremendous humility, it takes courage.

That seems wrong though, doesn't it? Stay with me on this. How many people do you know who follow their so-called "purpose" in life, then wake up one day floundering in a mid-life crisis? Or they realize they've wasted too many years following what others thought their purpose was.

Purpose, much like our very soul, was created specifically for us. Wonderfully crafted and remarkably unique. I thought my purpose was to play baseball, to become a professional athlete. How tragic for my life if this truly was the case! A mere chapter was to define my purpose? Thank God I was wrong.

Our dreams can die . . . our purpose cannot.

For professional athletes, transitioning into life after the game is one of the hardest obstacles we face. Everything changes, except you. Your routines change, your structure changes, your priorities change, your relationships change, your responsibilities change. Even your conversations change. Get the point? Here's the hard truth: You must re-discover yourself. You must identify three people:

—The person you were before
—The person you became
—The person you want to become

Believe me, I understand all too well the way the game makes you feel. It becomes our identity, confidence, and authority; however, it's only temporary. The time you spent playing is now over. Too many of us hold onto this short-lived identity far too long. If we don't lay the old dream to rest, it will continue to own us.

Face the Storm

What I had needed was a way to uncover the pain I kept deep down inside of me, a way to get it out. Many of us find ourselves lost not knowing "how" to fix the brokenness in us. But what's worse is when we do find out what needs to be done, many choose to NOT take the steps to fix it! I was willing to take the steps, but had to discover within myself if I was truly willing to pay the price.

Whatever I thought I had signed up for, I was wrong. It was beyond anything I could have imagined. For two years I had been following a men's program. I learned how to focus on the areas of importance in my life, to expect more from myself and to start living with intentional passion again. It had made a great impact but now was the time for the big commitment. Many of us say we are willing to "pay" any price for change, greatness, success. And yes, many pay the physical price. But only a small percentage of us are willing to pay the financial price. Talk is cheap, and many choose not to commit dollars to their personal growth. Bedros Keuilian said "Money is the filtration for the quality of the people you hang with."

In 2015, I learned that my level of success would be directly proportionate to the level of financial commitment I was willing to invest in myself. So when this "retreat" stared into my heart and mind, I knew I needed to pay the financial price.

Day one, I realized this was not a men's retreat, this was hell week and I was now fully entrenched in it. However, this would turn out to be the "come to Jesus" moment I never knew I needed. This was the scolding from the coach after a hard loss and the pep talk before a tough game all wrapped into one. This would coalesce what I thought I understood about my life's purpose into my most profound moment of clarity.

I remember in vivid detail, sitting in the cold, wet sand, huddled by four grown men. Crying through my pain and resentment, I spoke my question aloud . . . *the* question. The one question I was so afraid to ask all of these years. Why? Because I was afraid of the answer, the truth that could be revealed. To expose the story I had convinced myself to be true. My question was simply this: "Why . . . why did you take away the one thing you created me to become?"

I had no expectation of an answer, nor perhaps was I deserving of one. But the answer was given without hesitation, without pause. And in the most calming and heartfelt words, He spoke to me and said:

"I did not create you for baseball. It is but a chapter in your life, a story that you will use to have impact in the lives of others. Joshua, I have created you for so much more."

I still get emotional when I read it. That moment became the turning point in my life. It freed me of the burden I had felt every day after the game was over. It renewed my soul to believe I could become someone worthy of greatness in my life again.

There has to be a point where *you* experience your enough-of-this-shit moment. It only comes from the compounding of many small thorns in your side. Many scars earned, many failures notched. How many more thorns do you need to experience before you have your enough-of-this-shit moment?

After "hell" week, I had a new hunger—everything I had been taught, challenged to do, and motivated to attempt now had meaning. Yes, the jersey was off; however, I no longer saw myself as a "failed" professional athlete. I was determined to go all in and was going to war to discover myself again.

Clarity

In his book, *Play the Man*, Mark Batterson talks about chasing your lion, your biggest and scariest dreams. "Without a vision, a man will waste his life away. But with a clear vision, he's a force to be reckoned with. Because a true man is born for the storm."

After all my years of searching, reading, praying and asking for an answer, to experience that day was life giving! The forgiveness I was searching for. The clarity I was seeking. All were given in those few simple and profound sentences. Batterson's book reaffirmed this pivotal point in my journey. "Playing the man is playing offense with your life, your marriage, your faith."

Ready to take a stand, I was building the foundation to begin chasing in my life again. There was no more playing defense in my life. I realized if I wanted to change who I was, chase who I wanted to become,

I needed to start playing offense again. I had to stop believing in what others said to me that didn't align with my new goals and start believing in a vision of a man yet to be. I needed to "play the man" as I started to pursue the man.

Maybe like the old me, you have been too complacent in your life and allowed the excuses you tell yourself or the naysayer's comments to dictate who you have become. Many people attend seminars, read books, but don't take any further action. This is where most people stop and is a clean indicator they are not fully committed to the next steps. This is no longer acceptable. It's time to step up to a new plate, stand on a new mound.

When you realize this truth, your passions reveal your values, your values reveal your purpose, and your purpose reveals your life's meaning; you can't help but start chasing. I hope you are now realizing everyone has the power to change, pursue and to dream again! And you really should be terrified of the path you are about to walk because it is going to take someone very different than the person you are today to accomplish the journey.

> *Because you have a destiny that nobody else can live but you . . . so start living it.*
>
> —Sr. Miriam James Heidland

CHAPTER 5

Forgiving the Failure

The Weight of Shadows

As I think about the heartaches I carried for many years after the game was over, I can only describe it as a divorce. Early in the book I position our infatuation with our sport as a "significant other." Let's unpack that here. I've had a few close friends who experienced the intense pain of divorce. Looking back at my own pain, it correlates to having a spouse walk in one day and simply say: "I no longer love you. I'm leaving, and I'm taking the kids." What choice do you have at that moment? Your entire life walking out on you. What you love so intensely, stripped away.

Talk about a gut punch. Utterly helpless, you feel like the world is literally caving in all around you. You feel numb, and yet, your senses go into overdrive, creating this sick feeling in your stomach that never seems to go away. You know that feeling you get in your gut as the rollercoaster rounds the top of the incline and drops you recklessly down the other side so that you end up whipping along the track? When the game or the chapter ends, you go about life but as soon as the memory subsides, it pops up for no apparent reason and at the most inopportune times. At night in bed, it grinds away at your mind forcing you to relive every uncomfortable situation. Every mistake you made, every decision you should *have* made. Everything you couldn't, but somehow, should have controlled.

I have never experienced divorce in a marriage. But when the game left me, it left me broken, damaged, and wounded like a divorce wounds a family. It took everything. It turned its back on me, and so I turned my back on it. When you leave your sport or career, it doesn't care about you; it continues to flourish, and moves on without you.

There are many things we choose to not talk about when the door shuts. So we keep them locked away and held deep inside us never to be seen. We all have a black box. The only time the lid gets cracked open is when we put things in it. Heaven forbid we expose its contents in any way. Some of you may struggle with this idea. I did. It's something I avoided my entire life, and for good reason.

When you open the lid, understand you are about to go to war with your own mind. All your doubts, all your fears will be revealed. All your weaknesses, your insecurities, the resentments you've held onto, the darkness that trails along behind you—everything you are hiding from the world will be unveiled in its ugliest form . . . your truth.

You must learn to embrace the darkness in your past. If you ache to truly move on and discover everything you can become, you must face both the shadows of your past and your current reality. If you choose to continue to run away and avoid this onerous process, you'll never be able to live in the light.

You must come face-to-face with all the regret, excuses, lies, hurt, and failures lingering there. This is brutally painful because they bear all the shame you feel from your major failures and decisions. If you had succeeded, it would have been dismissed, considered acceptable and even a part of what makes you unique and special. But you didn't succeed, and so, they impose an even heavier weight on your life.

This deadweight would be my cross to carry for years. Mine alone to bear because it was hidden, never in view of anyone else. I could hardly let any of the shame I bore daily become even greater by exposing imperfections other people could see! No way! I wasn't about to go there. Never would it have occurred to me that in order to no longer be afraid of what I had so expertly hidden—all that unforgivable failure—I had to face, embrace, and take ownership. I had to forgive myself for it. Forgiveness isn't shedding ownership or blaming outside factors. It's walking right into the face of the problem, and owning it.

In order for the seeds of some trees and plants to germinate, they need to be exposed to fire so the resin encapsulating their seeds can melt away. Much like these seeds, your black box has a layer of resin encapsulating it. It's time to light the fire to burn it off!

Taming the Beast

Shame is not the same as guilt; it's a different kind of animal. Shame creates a completely different level of pain in your life. Guilt is one thing. People feel guilty all the time for the mistakes they make. When you feel guilt, you experience regret for having done something bad. But shame would have you believe you *are bad* for something you did. As this process of opening your black box uncovers the guilt in your life, as well as the shame, you must understand the difference.

It's not easy to forgive yourself when you believe that you are bad because of something you did or failed to do. We, then, often turn to blame. We blame others for our failure. We deflect with blame and transform it into anger to mask the pain (self preservation at it's finest). This anger is often brought out in misguided ways—living it out in our personal lives with those who are closest to us. We commit ourselves to the most damaging mix—shame and blame together. So desperate to get out from underneath the misery of shame, we hurl blame as a quick fix.

Fear of not being enough drives us into this feeling of shame. How could anyone see good inside of us? There were moments in my life when I suffered my biggest insecurities, not because they were justified but because, at those moments, I felt trapped and ended up giving in to my weakest view of myself. Feeling vulnerable, feeling unworthy, needing reassurance, but never knowing how to communicate it properly. Typically, I'd resort to what felt natural—jealousy, envy, bitterness, and self-pity. I would end up doing the exact opposite of what I truly needed to do, which was to reach out for help.

Shortly after I proposed to Kate, her folks came out from Kansas to help us figure out our wedding plans. As a guy, you aren't expected to be particularly interested in the fine points of wedding planning. But I was all in for it—logistics are right up my alley. I was having a tough time in my career; I'd just been cut from the Colorado Rockies. My arm still wasn't 100 percent, but I was not about to give up on my career. My finances were stretched, and that is putting it nicely. Credit card debt was piling up. I was living beyond my means. I had created an unrealistic image of success. And Kate knew it.

Kate has always been the saver in our relationship. I had never seen any reason to save money. I was going to make millions! And of course, I felt I was destined to make it. So why couldn't everybody just relax? We had a hard conversation about this just days before her parents arrived. I solemnly promised to not put another dime on my credit card.

Well, Kate's dad and I took her car to run some errands, and of course, it was running on empty. So we pulled into a gas station, and lo and behold, I didn't have enough cash to fill her tank. That conversation with Kate was fresh in my mind, and I was determined to be the *good* fiancé and keep my promise. I put $10 of gas in her tank using my debit card. The look on my future father-in-law's face said plenty about what he thought of his daughter's husband-to-be. Humiliating myself in front of Kate's father was just about as unbearable as having just been let go from my dream team. That moment became a lasting impression in his mind—I was an unfit choice and not the right man for his daughter.

How could this be? Growing up, I *was* the boyfriend every parent wanted their daughter to marry. Somehow, I had even managed to ruin that part of who I was. Years would pass before her parents would see me as a man worthy of their daughter. It was devastating for me, but in reflection, who could blame them? Maybe they saw the broken man I was that nobody else seemed to be seeing. Or maybe their lack of belief in me was exactly what I needed to see and feel for myself. Maybe it's what I needed in order to start showing up in my own life.

Her father, John, and I now have a great relationship, for which I am grateful, and that is true of both of her parents. Our children love their grandparents more than anything. It may have taken many hard conversations and tons of grace on both sides, but not a day goes by where I am not happy for all of it—I regret none of the past nor the resolve it took to get here. Now that I have two daughters, you'd better believe the process of giving their hands in marriage will be a thorough one. And I'm pretty sure I know a guy who can help me with that.

The Right Relationship

Earlier we spoke about rebar and how it makes for a solid foundation. Without a solid foundation, your support system will fail. Unfortunately, we screw this up and make people the rebar in our foundation. The hard truth is that people will fail you; they will come and go. People are just as imperfect as you are. It's not good or bad, it just is. People will let you down; they will walk away. No human relationship that you build will last forever. I know that sucks but think about it. Every day we are one day closer to our death.

The most important relationship I discovered on my journey was the one with God.

Everything you will need—the strength, forgiveness, grace, grit, endurance, peace, and the vision—will come from this relationship.

The many conversations you will need to have in order to become this person you so desperately want to become will all start with Him and you. While there are many truths and important ideas to take ownership of in this book nothing else truly matters if you do not embrace this truth and trust this part.

We Are All Broken

I spent thirteen years of my life allowing my failures to own me. Searching for ways to release them, to leave them behind, never coming close to understanding how to take ownership of them.

When we compete, train, and carry high standards within the realm of our personal expectations, it becomes impossible to look at life in the same manner. Our experiences are now different, our thoughts are different, and our reactions toward others are different. It's not that we see ourselves as better, but different, absolutely. The sacrifice, the pain, the mental fortitude, the relentless pursuit—the entire effort shapes who we are and what we expect of ourselves and others.

When you demand yourself to perform at such a high level (as you once did every single day), everything about you changes. When you fail, regardless of why you failed, the issue you face is how to forgive yourself. You have to forgive in spite of the nagging idea that you recklessly wasted your God-given talents, and you have to look ahead. Instead, believe you were created for far greater things than this chapter in your story.

Somewhere along the journey, I had convinced myself I was the only person out there who was broken, dealing with scars nobody could see. That somehow my brokenness was different. WE ARE ALL BROKEN! Whether we have external scars or internal, we are *all* broken in some way.

I use the word *broken* not as an excuse or to suggest insignificance but to identify that we all have a past; we all have a story of heartbreak, of loss, of defeat and sorrow. And that is exactly the point! It takes being aware of these various levels of pain, in order to see that you are stronger than you think and capable of so much more than you believe. You and I are amazingly unique, but we are not alone. I tried to convince myself that no one had gone through what I had. *No one feels the way I do inside. How could anyone relate to my struggles?* Sound familiar?

So why do we feel this way? We have a debt that we owe ourselves. We have a debt that we owe others. Until we repay the debt, it will stand in our way of growth. So, if we have a debt that we believe cannot be repaid, how are we supposed to carry that burden?

Taking Ownership

There came a time in my life when the bill came due, and I needed to get a hard look at exactly what debt I had racked up. I needed to get a good look at the many skeletons in my closet—all the regrets I had clung to, all the hurt I had blamed myself for, all the carnage I had created in my life, and all the collateral damage for which I was responsible. What I needed was a hard and honest conversation with myself.

This conversation took place once I finally came face-to-face with this reality of living a lie that became my life. I had to admit the type of person I had been was not who I am. I needed to come to terms with the fact I was 100 percent responsible for the damage I created in my life and the lives of others. Only then could I begin to have that honest conversation and start the healing process. The transformation out of our old self consists of many moments.

People heal by asking for forgiveness in several different ways. For me, it meant engaging in a brutal, heart-exposing confession. For others it's righting the wrongs they committed. I needed to eradicate the dishonesty in my life. It's about taking out your personal trash.

Monsignor O'Neil, a man of tremendous grace, heard my confession. Painful, yet liberating—I found a way at last to put my childish, selfish past behind me. All the mistakes and stupid decisions were revealed, and now forgiven. I began to heal inside, and the new man began to take shape and unveil himself. I still had so many questions, so many hurdles to cross. There were other people from whom I needed to seek forgiveness. And ultimately, from myself. But I started. That's the hardest part. There are a million reasons not to do this, but only one reason to do it. You need to let that single reason be stronger than any of the others.

First, separate the debt. This is the literal act of organizing the trash you've been harboring. Get it in order so when you deal with it, you can take it one piece at a time. The ultimate failure you hold onto is between you and that specific failure. The other debts—the hurt, lies, and guilt—need to be sorted. You want to be freed of these debts? Then make them right. Take ownership and have those conversations you need to with the people you feel need the closure. You need to do this so you can release the debt you carry.

If you can't have that conversation with them, then you need to find a proxy. Find someone who can stand in for them, someone you trust and who knows your heart and conviction to make it right. And with complete humility, apologize, take ownership, and ask for forgiveness. See, when we are able to release the debt we owe others, we literally take the weight of that pain off our own hearts. Until then, we consume ourselves with questions we can't possibly answer: *Can they forgive me? Will they forgive me? Can I forgive myself?*

Is it time to release this debt in your life, to let go of the burden around your neck, and begin to stand upright with the courage to face your next challenge, to find this better you?

At the age of thirty-five, my life took a much-needed shift in direction. By this time, my career had taken off. I had a real estate team, and we were successful in our local market. I had built my reputation back to what I believed was worthy of being considered successful, and my family was growing. By now, Kate and I had three children with one on the way—Caden, Brady, Maddy, and soon to be, Grace. I began to accept the reality that this was my new life, and that even though my life was good, I would never experience the feeling of achieving my true purpose.

How many of you recognize that you have gotten to this place in your life—where the new you is partially alive? Moments of bliss would come and go. It was easier and easier to become complacent as I sedated myself with work, distractions, and a litany of other deflections. They were enough to get me through another day, another week, another year.

How could I have settled for so little?

Though I had become resigned to accepting this was now my truth, deep down, I couldn't believe this was it. This was *not* how my life was supposed to turn out! I was a successful real estate agent, had a great family, and was doing great . . . on the outside. It's not that I wasn't grateful; I knew I was blessed beyond measure to have my health, a family, work, all the things we ask for in life. Happiness doesn't come from outside factors. It comes from within. True happiness cannot be lusted after, it must be cultivated and grown.

Have you ever wondered? What if the walls I put up in my life were not there to protect me? What if they were there to stop me from truly living my life? What if everything that happened to me had actually been happening for me?

I started having more conversations with God. I had never realized that in all my years I was such a terrible listener. It was always me doing the talking, me doing the pleading, me making suggestions, me creating the story as well as the answers to the questions I was wanting to hear. It became uncomfortably apparent I needed to change my conversations with Him.

First, these sessions had to become my appointments with Him. Why an appointment? Because if I made the appointment, I had to show up. He was always going to be there. It was simply a matter of whether I was choosing to show up. This is a change in understanding that many of us need to make.

Second, I started talking less, and listening more. Every morning, I have this ritual, this appointment, this opportunity to hear Him in my life. When's the last time you simply shut up and listened? You know what practice feels like. Practice listening.

A Door of Possibility

As this spark of newfound curiosity started to consume me, I found myself questioning everything in my life. Where else in my life was I settling? Was I truly good with being just *good*? Do my kids deserve a good dad? Does Kate deserve a good husband? Do my companies deserve a good leader? Do I deserve a good life? What if I simply were to change just that one word to *great*, how could my life look? The door of possibility started to nudge a little, and I was about to blow it open; you can, too. It starts with a simple shift in the way you view the journey, your potential, and ability to chase something new.

So, if life was happening *for* me, what was I supposed to be learning and why? All these areas in my life that hadn't been developed were now being exposed to me as crutches for my lack of success. I needed to respond to this growing awareness.

I needed to identify specific areas in my life where I was failing. I needed to create disciplines in my life, in order to conquer these areas where I was no longer willing to play the losing role. In my marriage, I would start to have conversations with Kate about how I could be the great husband she deserved and needed me to be. See it doesn't matter what I think she needs. If I'm not fulfilling her needs and desires, then it's a losing proposition.

I started to ask men in my life what a great father looks like. I would work to learn from their experiences. I would communicate with Kate, and take steps to follow through on our talks. In business, I became extremely intentional in building up our leaders and having uncomfortable conversations. Helping them achieve their goals would, in turn, help the company achieve its goals. I began to recognize the disciplines needed in my life actually had a deeper meaning.

Still, it wasn't enough. I was missing a key component. Months passed, and though great momentum was created, I was burning out. I was pouring out to so many people, depositing into so many lives, my own cup was running dry. It's easy to forget to take care of yourself when this journey gains traction. It's easy to let it consume you and get lost in it. Make sure you remember this journey is about leading others, but it begins by leading yourself first.

I began to lead in so many areas of my "outside" life, but forgot the one area I needed to lead in first—mine. For many years, I selfishly pursued my dream. It was all about me and accomplishing my goal. When it was over and humility finally slapped me in the face, I put myself on the back burner and ignored trying to *lead myself.*

Have past failures convinced you that you are not worthy of leading yourself? If we hold onto this belief, we cannot live in any of the disciplines we know we need in our lives. Instilling discipline in our lives actually gives us the freedom we have been searching for. It gives us back the power we lost. It restores control.

We have this false narrative about *discipline.* In our culture, it has become a concept associated with punishment. But if we could understand the possibilities when discipline is woven into our daily activities, we would begin to experience the ultimate freedom from guilt and regret. We are at our best when we live in our disciplines.

Knocking Down Your Walls

If you had everything you wanted, you might have missed what you really needed. Had I accomplished my dream of reaching the major leagues, I would have missed out on what I really needed. Years ago, there's no way you could have convinced me of that. Yet, with every day that passes, I become more and more convinced of this truth. I still believe

God's grace in my life would have protected me; however, I also know I am merely a man and a flawed one at best.

There are many things I needed in my life, and baseball covered up most of them. It revealed many of my greatest attributes, but also uncovered many of my biggest weaknesses. I am a better man because of the game and am becoming an even better man after the game. Baseball played a significant role in my life. Even though I buried it for far too long, it always remains, no longer a crutch but as a catalyst for me to discover who I will become.

So . . . what if it's not final? What if the walls you put up in your life were built not to protect you, but to stop you from truly living your life? *What if everything that has happened to you in your life has actually been happening for you?*

Isn't it time you gave up the crutch, the addiction, the distractions in your life? That story you keep convincing yourself to believe? Isn't it time to start putting the disciplines back where they belong? Isn't it time your life started to model the person you know you want to be? Isn't it time to lead yourself so you can experience freedom and control again? Yes. It is time. It's time to start knocking down those walls.

CHAPTER 6

Power of Presence

Search Mission

What's the story you keep convincing yourself to believe? How long have you taken ownership of it? Is now the right time to start putting the disciplines back where they belong? Is now the right time in your life to start modeling the person you know you want to be? Is now the right time to lead yourself, so you can experience true and lasting freedom and control?

Seriously, what's with all the questions?! Not many of us have people in our lives who are willing to go "there" with us. To ask the hard questions and dig deep past the superficial crap. We've numbed ourselves too quickly, in order to bypass deep and meaningful conversations with people, with our spouses, with our friends.

How many of you know a good friend who has been divorced, battled a major life decision, or lost a family member, and then when you found out, you felt blindsided and were caught wondering why you didn't know sooner? Or maybe you were the one going through hard times and felt like you had no one to turn to. Many of us have lost the confidence in others and ourselves to build deep and meaningful relationships. We didn't develop the tools or see the importance of these relationships—until we found ourselves backed into a corner we couldn't get out of.

For many years, I battled these emotions. I spent a long time wallowing in self-doubt. I didn't need anyone else to help fulfill my insecurities about who I *wasn't* anymore. It's not that I didn't have a supportive wife, an amazing father, and others who were in my life trying to help. I just didn't know how to let them. The self-help genre in the world is growing faster than ever before, but there wasn't anything I could find that spoke to me. I searched and absorbed everything I could. I was just trying to figure out who I was meant to be. But everywhere I turned, I felt like I was striking out.

Authority

When I was growing up, my dad was always around. There wasn't a day after school that he wasn't home to play catch, throw the ball, or wrestle with us. He was constantly pushing us to do more and become more. Pushing us to expect more from ourselves. Which was exactly what I wanted and yearned for. At the time however, I didn't know just how blessed I was to have a father like him. I grew up thinking every father was like my dad. I was completely naive and oblivious to how the real world actually worked.

Pushing us came pretty easy to him as a former collegiate athlete, in fact, an all-American basketball player. As I was growing up, my dad was young enough to still be playing pick-up games in rec leagues. I was not only able to hear him speak that courage into my life, I was able to see him apply it through his love for sport as well.

Some of my fondest memories were of watching him drop 40 to 50 points on guys half his age. He had the sweetest shot and crazy hops for a 5'11" white dude! He was quick and agile and was a student of the game. Basketball was his classroom. There is no doubt that the passion I have in my life came from him and how he attacks his.

As devoted to his sport as he was, the most important devotion in his life has always been his pursuit of serving God. Most people would

STRIKE THREE

read that text and think, "Not his family, not his wife or his children?" Not a day has gone by that we as a family ever questioned his love for us. His strength came from his priorities, and there is no doubt that he was the dad he was to us because of his love for the Lord.

There were many times when he would miss one of his own basketball games or one of our sporting events because he was serving, leading, or participating in ministry. Because of this, we were actually empowered to know our value in his eyes, and His eyes.

Too many men, too many marriages, are too busy being just ok, average, ordinary. As Francis Chan said, "If your marriage is just about fun or being happy, then it's worthless." Whoa, worthless? You'd better believe it. Every man, woman, and marriage has been given a divine authority in their lives and in their children's lives. How are you living out this authority that has been given to you?

My father always knew of this authority and he has spent his life discovering how to fulfill it. He cared more about improving himself in the areas that truly mattered, like being a better father, husband, man, than by attending a game, a function, or a practice. He wasn't ignoring his family; he was setting the example for us to follow. It was an affirmation of how much a dad should love his family. He was willing to sacrifice to become a better father, husband, and man in the important areas of his life.

He modeled in real life what he taught. He has always been a man who challenged himself and took personal responsibility. That model was set before me every day to embody and repeat. And it's a good thing he did. As my life would be tempted, distracted, and eventually broken, it would be because of he and my mothers foundation that I would be drawn back home both physically and metaphorically.

So why do I share this side of my life with you? I've come to realize how important planting seeds in our children is. As I left home to pursue my dreams no matter how far I strayed away from the child I was, I had parents who never gave up. They always believed in who I was capable of becoming. This young man that they were raising would lose his way, his identity, but never their love and constant prayers. They believed one day I would find *me* again. That I would discover who I was supposed to become because they always saw him in me, especially when I didn't anymore. Are there seeds that you need to start planting in the lives of those you are influencing? Don't waste another day waiting on someone else to plant the seeds you've been given.

Never Again

Looking back at my childhood, I see many failures and many losses. I hated losing! It was extremely personal to me. Losing was a reflection of my own value even back then. When we lost our seventh-grade basketball championship, I was wrecked for over a week. I remember writing a report about how much losing sucks! Ha ha, seriously, I have to laugh because the emotions still come back after all these years, and I find myself justifying why I was so passionate about winning and losing.

When the game was over, so was this competitive spirit I had harnessed over my lifetime. While growing up, I heard stories of Hall of Fame athletes that refused to lose, at anything. Stories of Cal Ripken Jr. and Michael Jordan convey how these athletes wouldn't let anyone beat them at ANYTHING! As a young kid and "future" Hall of Famer, I wasn't going to break this tradition.

It was the end of my freshman year, and I was about to embark on my high school career. The award for athlete of the year was to be handed out that evening. Going into that night I had imagined walking up to the podium to receive this award. The speech was already written in my head, and the only thing that needed to be done was for my name to be announced. Have you ever seen the movie where the guy goes up to the stage to receive the award that he didn't win only to find out that someone else was the winner? I was that guy. As the winner's name was announced I literally almost stood up but somehow had the willpower to stay seated while realizing the reality of what just happened. I just lost. I just lost the award! My world crumbled around me, and the only thing I remember afterwards was being home in the workout room, taking my scrawny self through a punishing workout to get all my anger and frustration out.

My father would eventually come in, and the only words I would say to him were, "Never again, never again, will I give up control whether I win or lose." It was a pivotal moment in my career, it was a defining moment for the intestinal fortitude I would need as I battled to make something of myself.

From then on, I refused to lose at anything I did. And if I happened to lose, you'd better believe I was practicing even harder in order to be ready for the next game. It didn't matter what it was, ping-pong, basketball, beer-pong! Yes, yes, I said that. Remember, I was a starting pitcher. Pitching every fifth day allows for a lot of other activities between starts. I wasn't going to let you beat me at anything. Even beer pong!

Two Beasts

I've come to realize we all have two beasts inside of us. I've always been drawn to lions. So, when I think of these beasts inside of me, I picture two lions. One is magnificent and reflects the best in who we are and want to be. When we feed this beast by giving selflessly, we build up others, we lead from the front knowing we are pouring into others. I have a phrase that I say "Empty the tank, everyday in every way." More on this later in the book but understand this now, we must choose to empty *our* tanks in the important areas of our lives. When I walked away from baseball, I left the healthy competitive spirit in the locker room and started feeding the wrong inner beast.

Understand, I was still competitive, still passionate, but not in the same way as before. Now it was out of bitterness and resentfulness. It was out of frustration. This is a different lion in me, in all of us. It wasn't about succeeding or bettering myself or others; it was about holding on to the past, trying to gain false self-worth. This beast inside us all brings out the qualities that, when we are not healthy, can be destructive. When we see our life unfulfilled then our outlook on the same situation is completely different. The good qualities become our worst qualities. The dark beast inside me that I couldn't control was being loosed.

As I began my career in real estate, one of the mistakes I made was that work never stopped. I fed this false belief that my clients needed me more than my wife or soon-to-be family. Easily justifying it, I would break promises, miss birthdays, events, and time with Kate in our early years. One of my most regrettable memories of my mismanaged moments and feeding the wrong beast was the day our first child, Caden, was born. I was working relentlessly to become a *success*. It didn't matter what it was professionally, I needed to experience that feeling of self-worth again, and real estate was that avenue.

Caden was born in the early morning hours of November 20, 2007. As we welcomed in this handsome, bleached-blonde little guy (better highlights than I ever had, and his were natural!), I received a message mid-morning that I needed to show a property to a potential client. Now understand that I had been living with this regret that maybe, just maybe I hadn't worked hard enough, had given up too soon on myself, or quit just a little too early chasing my biggest dream. I wasn't about to experience that failure again. The memories of my ninth-grade year combined with my most recent "loss" were haunting me. I was not going to lose at anything ever again. I would pay any cost. And because of this motto I would test every relationship I had going forward, losing some and testing others to the breaking point.

So early that morning I left to work. I showed my clients properties that day and left Kate and Caden at the hospital as I "played the man." Long before I understood what "being" the man truly meant. Another fail . . .

STRIKE THREE

Tell the Truth

Through my many ups and downs, faults and failures, my father was a constant rock in my life. He'd be the first to give me a bear hug after a loss or to cheer me on after a victory. But of all the lessons he instilled in me, one of the most important was his conviction, as a father, to always tell me the truth. Painful, yet necessary, moments. I knew I would always have a fan in him, but I was also going to have someone there to give me a reality check.

What a concept—tell the truth! If we, as a culture, could just sit, ponder, and implement this novel idea, how different would our world be? Heck, let's just start with our families, our marriages, ourselves. I had never realized, prior to this, how powerful this principle could be in my life! As I learned to tell the truth in my life, I started to apply it in all areas. But the most important one, the one that made the biggest impact was learning to expect nothing but the truth from myself. When I could look at a situation and not buy into the story I would tell myself. Or the misguided belief of why they were wrong and I was right, my world opened up to a new reality. An interesting thing started to happen. The beast I'd been trying to harness, control and temper started to realize he no longer controlled me. I became the master of my inner beasts.

Has the shift started to happen for you yet? In the previous chapter I asked you to take a hard look at your life, has that view become more clear? Your marriage? Your health? Your work? It's often not as good as we think. Things are not as our Instagram posts would indicate. Like you, I lied to myself and to others for years. I couldn't tell the truth because I didn't even know what the truth was.

Instilled in you and me at a young age was the notion that we were meant to be more. We were part of the *1 percent*. We were not meant to be like everybody else. Our lives were not supposed to be average.

We were supposed to challenge ourselves and everything that we were capable of becoming.

Now, most books would take you in a direction and make a statement along the lines of the following: *Many of us have lived our lives as the 1 percent. The exception to the rule, the exception from everyone else. Reinforced from an early age by coaches, teammates, teachers, and our parents was this notion we were the 1 percent. That somehow because we had a talent, we were going to be propelled to higher levels of achievement in our lives. And so, we bought into it. Why wouldn't we? We loved our uniqueness; it's what drove us. It identified in us a strength that was ours alone. Being a part of the 1 percent made us special and singled us out only to make us stand out!*

Go find another book. I'm not here to talk to you about the 1 percent that made you stand out. This is not about your uniqueness; we've already covered that.

It's about the 1 percent you give away that's holding you back.

Most of us have this concept that we are giving 100 percent of ourselves. Whether in sports, business, or relationships, we believe we are giving more than 100 percent. How many coaches have told you to give 110 percent?! Love the motivation, but it's unrealistic. (Side note: I've been guilty of saying that exact same quote.)

Giving 100 percent? I'm here to tell you that you are not.

Take Back the 1%

For so much of my life, I was searching for an understanding of what it took to be a great dad. I knew there were concepts waiting to be learned that embodied this course of action. I knew there were great dads out there, and I wanted to join their ranks. Heck, I wanted to be a great husband and business leader, too. Mostly, I wanted to be a great man.

Men, listen up, because I'm talking directly to you right now. As a man, I *knew* I wasn't living up to *my* expectations in any of these areas.

STRIKE THREE

I did what I *thought* needed to be done; I was a good dad, husband, and businessman. But my life was far from being on fire!

When I say I wanted to be a great dad, it meant I wanted to be excited to get home, hug my kids, drop everything to play catch, get on the ground and wrestle with each one of them, all while enjoying every moment of it. I wanted to be able to slow things down in my head so I could be present and truly embrace that time. But I couldn't. Something inside of me was off. Something inside of me wouldn't let me go there.

When I say I wanted to be a great husband, it meant that I wanted to be the man to walk in the door to a wife who couldn't wait for me to come home. Who when I embraced her, would be so excited to have her husband home that she couldn't wait to get the kids to bed! I wanted to have my wife pursue me! To know that when she looked at me, she not only saw a man on fire, she was on fire for her husband!

When I say I wanted to be a great businessman, it meant I wanted to have my crap together financially. That I would be leading my employees, team members, and associates to greater achievements. That I would be making smart, sound business decisions and that I would have a clear vision for my future.

I believed I was giving 100 percent. In fact, I was convinced, at that moment, I was giving 100 percent of what I was capable. I was exhausted by the effort I was putting out. And even more so, *from the lack of return*. I felt like I was making deposit after deposit. How many of you understand exactly what I'm talking about? How many of you can appreciate being exhausted for giving all of yourself and pouring out to other people? How many of you come home exhausted, wake up exhausted, and don't know if you can give anymore?

I've addressed a number of critical topics in this book, but seriously, this is something you need to really pay attention to. This has been a game changer in my life—*the 1% challenge*. It truly took my marriage from good, to on fire. My fatherhood from good to life-changing. My role as a business owner to that of a leader (not a guy who simply signs the checks).

You aren't giving 100 percent. You, at most, are giving 99 percent. And to most of us, that sounds like it's more than enough. In fact, it seemed so to me. I could easily justify the idea that 99 percent was more than enough.

I remember going to a marriage class that taught us "Marriage isn't 50/50; it's 100/100." What the heck does that even mean? Is it like 110 percent? How do you even do that? Still, I absolutely loved the idea. In fact, my wife, Kate, and I were high-fiving each other saying, "Yes! That's right!" But neither of us had any real idea of what that might look like in our marriage.

Even if our best is giving 99 percent, we still hand over the 1-percent burden for others to carry. Understand, this 1 percent we give away is *the expectation that we will receive something back.* How many of you, when you do something wonderful or nice for your significant other, proceed to wait for that text, wait for those words of affirmation? How many of you who are in business and lead other people wait for loyalty in return, wait for gratitude for all that you've done in their lives? And if you don't get it, there is a seed of resentment?

I spent a lot of my life giving, in order to receive. I thought I was giving selflessly. I thought I was giving of myself fully. But I was always opening the door to the 1% I expected, demanded, and needed in return. It wasn't much! I didn't need a lot in return. Just some acknowledgment. Somebody to appreciate me. I just needed somebody to fill my cup.

And therein lies the problem. I've said it before but it bears repeating. People will let you down; people will fall short. Because we are human. And if you put the burden of the 1% on them, you will always be disappointed. It is so freeing when you come to this realization: **You need to give with no expectation of anything in return.** When you are truly able to give fully with no expectation of return, it doesn't matter

STRIKE THREE

what happens. You'll never have to rely on others to fill your cup. This sounds much easier than it is.

No longer needing my kids' approval, I was now able to become the dad I wanted to be. No longer chained by my expectations nor what I needed to receive back from Kate, I could now become the husband I desperately wanted to be for her. I began leading in my businesses because I ceased searching for gratification. I was free to give unconditionally and unapologetically!

Once I realized how unrealistic it was for me to expect everyone else in my life to carry this burden, I had to take it back. I had to take back the expectations I was putting on people that were unfair and unjust. When I took back that 1%, I took back control of my happiness. I took back control of my future. I was no longer dependent upon the response I sought to elicit from others. What a relief! For the first time in years—since baseball—I felt a sense of purpose and direction.

For too many years, I lived with so much shame in my life. All I had been doing was trying to prove my worth—available only as affirmation from others. Even though I took on this concept of being unselfish by pouring into people, I was still dependent on others to confirm that what I was doing meant something.

You want to have an amazing marriage? Take back the 1%. You want to have an awesome relationship with your kids? Take back the 1%. You want to truly pour into the people in your life? Take back the 1%. You want to live a life on fire? Take back that 1%.

Start living!
Start leading!

CHAPTER 7

Impact & Influence

Qualified by Failure

During my career, I had this idea that when I made it to the big leagues, that's when I would become the teammate others would gravitate toward. That's when I would become an athlete of impact and influence. I had a clear image of this guy. The path was right in front of me. Yet farther than I could have ever imagined.

Many of us toppled from a high place and don't feel qualified to lead because of our brokenness. Here's the hidden truth. That's *exactly* why we are qualified. Our brokenness. A few years ago, Malcom Gladwell wrote *David and Goliath*. The premise of his book is this: Our biggest disadvantage can be leveraged as a massive advantage, allowing us to leap further ahead than those who presumably should be able to do more.

When we begin to realize our scars tell the stories that actually impact others, we begin to heal ourselves. This journey becomes bigger than us. We are able to harness strength when we realize pain is a connection in our lives. We can then build trust and rapport with others who have experienced shame, loss, pain, and hurt. Life is *always* working for you. It doesn't mean the pain is any easier or the loss any less significant. It just means life will use your brokenness to show you a greater future, if you are willing to see it.

It's easy to compare our failures, losses, stories, challenges to others. It's easy to allow our mind to convince us that our brokenness isn't worthy of sharing. Isn't worthy of healing. Isn't worthy of impact. I love to hear and read stories of those that overcome insurmountable odds in life to achieve greatness. Or how some of the most successful people found their greatness in the depths of destruction and loss. However, I can also find myself belittling my story, my pain, my brokenness because it is not like that of others.

If you find yourself doing this, just as I do to myself, STOP! Your mind will do everything it needs to do to keep you safe. To keep you from experiencing pain, discomfort, heartache. Just like me, your story is unique. Amazingly crafted, experienced, and lived like no other could have. Your thoughts, dreams, visions, losses, failures, victories, decisions, and motives are unlike anyone who has *ever* existed. I must remind myself that this journey is no longer about myself and my insecurities, but that I, just like you, were meant for so much more!

The Formula

For years, I've been praying a prayer over my kids that I heard after a Youth for Christ fundraiser I'd attended. The speaker that evening was a comedian that brought the house down with laughter, but more importantly, a powerful message. To this day, two things have stuck with me, and I have been trying to live them out ever since: *Are you passing away or passing on?*

1. We are meant not to be passing away but to be passing on. When my dream was over, I felt so much of my life had already passed away. Through this journey of self-discovery, I started to believe that somehow, someday, my past could be of value to people. It gave life to me again. It meant just maybe I could impart some truths I'd learned along the way and *that* would be of value. I began to internalize and believe I was made for more. I wasn't exactly sure for what, but I was going to find out.

2. The prayer. I have prayed a particular prayer over my children for the past number of years. Every night before they go to bed, it's our ritual. In fact, when traveling, I have called in or recorded it to be played prior to their bedtime. It is such a powerful prayer that has guided me as a father, and brought consistency and intentionality into my life. For your personal copy go to www.joshkalinowski.com for your free download.

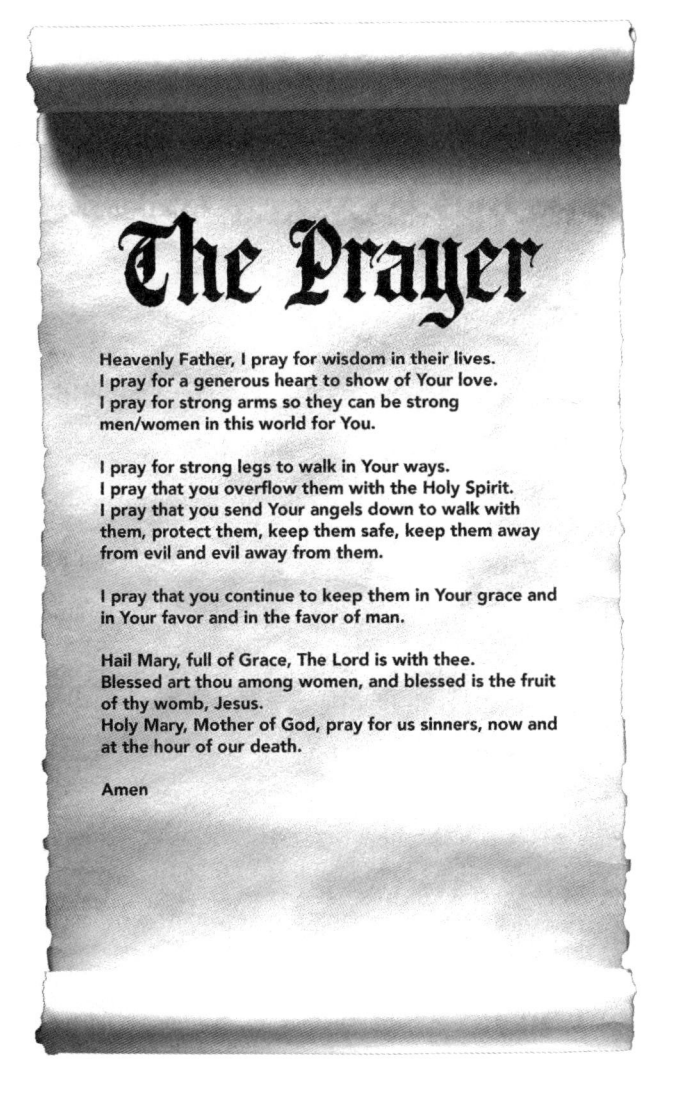

The Prayer

Heavenly Father, I pray for wisdom in their lives.
I pray for a generous heart to show of Your love.
I pray for strong arms so they can be strong men/women in this world for You.

I pray for strong legs to walk in Your ways.
I pray that you overflow them with the Holy Spirit.
I pray that you send Your angels down to walk with them, protect them, keep them safe, keep them away from evil and evil away from them.

I pray that you continue to keep them in Your grace and in Your favor and in the favor of man.

Hail Mary, full of Grace, The Lord is with thee.
Blessed art thou among women, and blessed is the fruit of thy womb, Jesus.
Holy Mary, Mother of God, pray for us sinners, now and at the hour of our death.

Amen

It wasn't until a number of months after that I sensed a tug on my heart, and a question popped into my head: *Why don't you pray this prayer over you?* It wasn't so much a question that needed an answer, but more the planting of a seed that would grow inside me. Eventually, it led me to say this as my daily morning prayer.

There are three things that resonate every time I say this prayer. *Wisdom, grace, and favor.* If you've ever prayed for a specific quality in your life, then you know that God will not give you the quality. Instead, He will give you the situations that will allow you to develop that quality. God wants you to be specific as well. If you are desiring a certain quality ask for it. However, be prepared to uncover, discover and be faced with opportunities to hone that quality in your life. As I pray for these and other specific qualities I have learned to embrace the opportunities He puts forth for me to sharpen my axe and become the man I desire to be. These become my integrity moments.

Wisdom, Knowledge, and Understanding

When asking for wisdom, I am fully aware that He is going to provide me with plenty of opportunities to gain knowledge and understanding in my life. Wisdom, on the other hand, will not magically appear. It is through experiences—trials, hardships, victories, and joy—that wisdom will be brought into my life. Unfortunately, God knows I learn the most when I fail. I still prefer trying to experience wisdom through victories and joy; it's a bit more fun! But I'm a work in progress.

One of the best ways to gain wisdom in your life is to sit at the feet of another. As I began my personal journey of self-discovery, I realized I needed to continue this theme of humility in my life but with a twist. I mistakenly thought that having humility in my life meant I needed to coward away from tough conversations, tough choices, or tough things. I convinced myself that being humble meant being weak. The truth is that humility in our lives is a sign of tremendous strength. It means that you are comfortable, confident in who you are, what you believe in, and what you stand for, regardless of what is being thrown at you. It is the understanding that the real battle is not with the other person but with controlling the beast inside of you that wants to destroy everything you've worked hard to become. Humility is one of the greatest strengths you can develop. When you do, you will begin to notice that the little things in your life will teach you the biggest lessons.

Creating specific disciplines in your life is the key to unlocking your biggest potential. When I'm living in my disciplines (and filling my cup is one of them), my emotions are working for me and not against me. I'm feeding the right beast. I'm successful at attacking each day. Yes, *attacking*! Don't mistake me when I say I'm successful each day. Understand, the more I push and attack, the more challenging the days become. But I must have the mindset that I need to be on offense. It's time you started showing up and playing offense.

There are a handful of books that have impacted me in such a way that literally changed the way I think and look at life. I would be remiss if I did not continue to share and give credit where credit is due. One of those books is Play the Man by Mark Batterson. I referenced him and his book earlier. It is equally just to share more insight. In his book, Mark helps light the fire for any man who has a pulse and desires more out of his life. I had just turned forty, and I had been uncovering and rediscovering the man inside of me for quite some time. I was capable, motivated, and full of desire, but didn't have the direction.

In one of his best chapters, Batterson makes the case for stepping up as a man in our lives. This resonated intensely and ignited heavy emotions within me. He finished his statement with a call to action: "Do it like your life depends on it. In other words, give it everything you've got. Don't just make a living. Make a life. Don't just earn a paycheck. Go after the passions God has put in your heart. Half-way is no way to live; you've got to go all in."

Even as I write these words, the hair on my arms stands up, my adrenaline starts to pump, and strong conviction flows through me to get up and run through a brick wall!

As we journey through the chapters of our life, it's easy to get caught up thinking we will never have the wisdom to be impactful. Wisdom is an intimidating word and an elusive one at best. When I think of people with wisdom, I think of King David, Gandhi, Mother Teresa, Abraham Lincoln, etc. Epic players! I don't believe any of us would try to categorize ourselves in those hierarchies; however, wisdom does not delineate.

The formula is simple, yet it is profound when applied in life.

$$(Knowledge + Understanding) \text{Reflection}^N = Wisdom$$
$$(K+U)R^N=W$$

The first step to gaining wisdom is the pursuit of knowledge. Knowledge comes from the idea that you must be hungry to learn and humble enough to pursue. Knowledge is found in books, podcasts, conversations, and silence. However, It isn't until you take this knowledge and gain understanding through experience that you can progress toward wisdom.

Understanding can be found only through experience, so your second act must be action. Once you have taken action, you will then receive understanding of whatever it is you have acted upon. This sounds all too easy, like getting a drink of water. It's not that easy (for some, finding water can be very difficult). I don't want to sound like I'm holding some secret key here and am a Shaman who can lead you to the light. I'm not. You have to be willing to go after the experiences and to take from them the learning that will inevitably present itself along the way.

From there, we transition to wisdom by reflecting on our experiences. Reflection is one of the most powerful tools we can use in our lives, if done correctly. Unfortunately, too often, we reflect with an attitude of negativity, ambushing any opportunity for growth in our lives. Once again, we need humility in our lives. We must put ourselves in the best position for growth through reflection. Reflection leads us to the ultimate goal of pouring this wisdom we have earned into others. It is a process we have to seek with an unwavering thirst because of the life it can bring. Think of a glass of water and the thirst it quenches. Your need for new understanding must match your need for a glass of water. Wisdom is the water to your life.

THE CYCLE TO GAIN WISDOM

KNOWLEDGE → UNDERSTANDING → WISDOM

We can all look back at our past selves and identify those moments when we would have loved to have had wisdom—*before* the experience was felt or the decision was made. Yet it's only through those trying times and disappointments we experience *who* we are being molded into. And only if we are willing to follow the process. Life *will* continue to throw you curveballs. If you have the strength to look back and learn the lessons, attaining wisdom becomes a reality. It has been through the many setbacks, the disapointments and the life experiences that I now refect upon in order to obtain greater wisdom in my life.

Sometimes, I still can't help but wonder, *what if?* What would life have looked like if things had worked out the way I wanted them to? If all my plans had turned out like I had imagined, dreamed of, and created in my head? Would I be the man I am today? Would Kate still be married to me? Would we have the children we have today? How different would life really look?

My standard response, for so many years, was that I was grateful to God for knowing me better than I knew myself. That somehow my weaknesses would have destroyed my marriage, my relationships, and my reputation. I know that seems harsh, but I saw it happen to so many athletes and friends. During that period, this was also my first line of defense. By admitting my weaknesses, I didn't have to take responsibility. I shuffled it off on God, but that only worked for so long. Eventually, I convinced myself that this story was true, and I became embittered by it. I took ownership of it, all while wearing this as a badge of shame.

Our Stories

It seems impossible to take ownership of the story we've told ourselves for so long. We've worn this badge that's continued to hold us back from knowing the real truth in our lives! What if all your experiences are exactly what you needed in order to create the person you are *meant* to be?

After baseball, the sentence I repeated was: "Everything I've gone through is exactly what *destroyed* the person I was *created* to become." This was my sentence both literally and figuratively. This became my story. How many of you are still there?

During one particular visit with a close friend and former teammate, we went out for drinks after the game that evening. He was pitching in the big leagues, and his team was in town facing the Colorado Rockies. As we sat in the corner booth at the bar, fans recognized a few of the players and

STRIKE THREE

approached the booth for autographs. The napkin and pen started going around the table. My heart was pounding and my hands started sweating. I thought, *What do I do?* Just the previous year, *I* was playing baseball, *wearing* the jersey, *and* signing autographs for kids to grandparents and everyone in between. The anxiety I felt in this moment was overwhelming. The napkin moved closer. I wanted to justify why I should sign that stupid napkin, but I knew I shouldn't. So, I didn't. I passed it along. I was defeated again and reminded of the *life* sentence I was living out. I still hadn't taken ownership of my story. I was still believing in the lie I was convincing myself of. It was time to tell the truth.

When I finally took ownership of my weaknesses and my insecurities, things began to change. When I owned my shame, it could no longer control me. The story I began to share became *my* story! Full of all the good, bad, pain, sorrow, redemption, awakening, and love.

Have you been able to tell the truth? Are shame, guilt, and the stories you've convinced yourself of true? Are they holding you back from letting others know the real you? When I lost that future me—that fictitious man on the mountain—I hid him deep down in the black box. I didn't want to be vulnerable or be exposed like that ever again. It wasn't worth the pain. So, I settled for average in too many areas of my life. In his book, *It Takes What It Takes,* Trevor Moawad talks about settling for average. "Who wants to be average? Average is the place in the middle. It's the best of the worst or the worst of the best." I *hate* average! Once I changed my story, realized I could not settle for average anymore in my life, and started to speak my truth, I buried that old me. A new man was being born.

I'm not gonna lie. There are days I still question whether it's worth it, this growing into a better person thing. The days when the pressure weighs on you, people lean heavily on you, people doubt you, leave you, talk about you. Some days, it seems easier to just keep my head down and mind my own business. Grind in my own life. Make the money and get to retirement. But then, I look at my kids and wife. I look at myself and all those I'm leading. I look at all of those who are leading *with* me. And that's when I'm reminded of exactly why I need to continue to fight for this man I'm chasing to become!

I chased money for too long. I chased a perfect lifestyle for too long. A perfect image of me for too long. I don't chase perfection anymore. I chase excellence! It's time to run down that brick wall of complacency and smash it!

> *Chase your passions like your life depends on it. Give it everything you've got. Don't just make a living. Make a life. Don't just earn a paycheck. Go after the passions God has put in your heart. Halfway is no way to live; you've got to go all in.*
>
> —Mark Batterson

CHAPTER 8

Finding Your Team

You Are Not Alone

We were never meant to do life alone. We were never meant to experience pain, hardships, joy, or peace without people around us. Have you ever wondered why you find so much joy in celebrating life with other people? Or why you find so much comfort in the company of others when hard times are upon you? It's because we are wired for community. We were created to experience life with others. So quit trying to do the hardest things in life alone.

For years, I would try to tackle the hardest situations in my life alone. As a man, as a leader, I felt I needed to do this by myself. To prove to myself and to others that I was strong and stoic—superhuman. I would shield others from knowing the truth about areas I was struggling in because that's what strong leaders do. I would isolate my loved ones from the struggles I was facing personally and professionally because I didn't want to burden them with my issues.

In 2015, the perfect storm was about to hit my life. I had been an owner of a real estate firm for nearly six years. And for the most recent three, I had been the sole owner, having bought out my business partner in 2012. We were growing as a company, but my vision was much bigger. I followed the simple rule; if it was *big*, it could be *bigger*!

As the vision for our company and my family grew, an opportunity to move on a building came forth. You have to understand where I was at mentally to appreciate why this was so important to me. Here I was finally breaking out of my shell of shame. Taking a chance to develop my new path as a *successful* entrepreneur. I was finally betting on myself again! This wasn't just another building—this was everything I believed I needed in order to become this new me!

In February of 2015, we broke ground on a 13,000 sq/ft complete renovation project. The future of Kalinowski Enterprises was upon us, and we were building another layer to our legacy, my legacy. Everything was gutted except the exterior walls, everything. You could literally see from one side of the building into every corner of the building and into the roof. Prior to our demolition, the building held over fifty offices, reception areas, multiple bathrooms, asbestos, mold, and tons of debris. It had been vacant for years; it was perfect!

Our current building measured 4,500 sq/ft. We were about to triple our square footage and our monthly overhead. But we were good. I had a strong anchor tenant, which I had just partnered with, the economy was great, and we were growing. We had purchased the building for a good price. The remodel cost was comfortably in our budget. Understand, my father was in construction for over thirty years, and I had been around the building trades my entire life.

This was right up our alley. In addition, I had budgeted roughly 20 percent overage in costs to protect us. The project was underway! Isn't it fortunate for us not to know the future? There are times when it would be beneficial. But generally, if we could know what we were about to get into, most of us would avoid the pain, the discomfort, the failure.

In June, things started to show signs of cracking. The foundation that I had been building on in my life was beginning to show its lack of rebar. The market was slowing, the project started to incur bigger expenses, and the anchor tenant exposed some financial issues that had not been disclosed before. But what do you do? Without knowing and with blind faith, you continue to move on and show up.

From the beginning of our relationship, Kate and I have worked hard to have an open and honest relationship with each other. For those of you who have been fortunate to find and keep someone so special, you realize there are many areas in which you complement each other. She is the best piece of my puzzle. Security has always been important to her. As an entrepreneur and former athlete, there has never been security in my life. Kate desires stability; I desire change. In any successful marriage, it takes time, experience, and grace to build and develop trust with each other. We were about to receive a lot of experience, and it would push the limits of our grace.

Coming Clean

At this point in my life, I didn't have any men, other than my father, who were sitting at my board table. I didn't even know I should be looking for people who could pour into my life, give me direction, encouragement, or just get me back in line. I didn't have mentors I could talk with and know they were holding me accountable to be the husband I had promised to be, the dad I was called to be, or the leader I desired to be.

As you are very aware by now, my father has been an amazing man in my life. Next to Kate, he is my best friend. He is one of my mentors, and it's because of his example, guidance, and love that I am who I am today. But what I didn't realize or appreciate is that you shouldn't have just one person giving you guidance in your life. This is where having a board table in your life is of the utmost importance. And at this crucial time in mine, I had no one else to guide me.

You need to think of your life as if you were building a company. Think about the structure and the foundation of how you design the hierarchy, the chain of command, and the ways in which you gather information, make decisions, evaluate future moves, deal with issues, and vision cast. When everything hits the fan and all hell breaks loose, who would you involve, who would you turn to, who would you trust to be honest with you?

Once you have identified them you need to invite them to your board. I have included additional resources that you can use to invite your board members. You are the owner and CEO; who would you want on your board? You need to fill these positions: your COO, CFO, advisors, and mentors. You can find a list of questions and specific resources that can be used to identify your board members at www.joshkalinowski.com. The idea is to create a board that will help you become the very best in three specific areas: business, health, and life.

(Diagram: A circular board table with positions labeled CEO, CFO, BOARD MEMBER, BOARD MEMBER, BOARD MEMBER, COO around the perimeter, with "BOARD TABLE" in the center.)

I was simply trying to show up and do my best. But once again, my best wasn't going to be good enough. I remember the moment like it was yesterday. I was sitting in our new building, in my new office. Looking

STRIKE THREE

out of my new window onto our new parking lot and wondering how long could I keep this up! The market had stalled. We were now a quarter of a million dollars over budget, the bank accounts were dwindling—and Kate had no clue. I was trying to protect her from my burden, but the truth of it was, I did not want to hear her saying, "I told you, I told you not to do this!"

Back in 2014, when I cast this vision of what our future could look like with this new building, Kate hesitated. She stalled, but I kept going. Convinced that this was our future, certain this was meant to be. Certain, I knew best.

But when things started to stall out, all my past emotions of shame rushed back into my life at that moment. I'm about to fail. . . again. Not again, please not again! On the brink of losing everything, or so it seemed, I did what I didn't do the last time. I didn't walk away, bury my head, or leave. I stood my ground. I faced my fears. Falling to my knees, I confessed everything to Kate, came clean on the decisions I had been making, took 100 percent responsibility for everything, and asked for forgiveness. I took back the 1 percent!

I would make tough calls to the bank, just in case I needed a plan. I would be humbled again, but this time, I would find my strength. I would find my resilience and would solidify what I was willing to fight for. I would not waste the previous decade-long struggle and lessons learned along the way to start all over again. You'll notice the immense use of the word "I" in this paragraph. This is how we own our story. This is how you build integrity within yourself. This is how you start believing in yourself. This is how you go from where you are to where you want to be!

From that moment on, we began to climb out of the hole I had created. Progress was grueling and slow at first, but it was progress nonetheless. It was painful, but Kate would forgive me, more importantly, she would stand by me. Our relationship was forged tighter through that chapter of our life. 16 years and counting, stronger by each passing struggle, closer with each victory. Kate is now the CFO at my board table, and I have added a COO, mentors, and advisors. Though the pain of those decisions I had made sucked for a period of time, they solidified my marriage and grew me as a husband and as a man. I found out what I was willing to fight for and how much I needed to change, in order to become who I wanted to be.

It's Possible

After I started to put the pieces together, I realized how important these areas of my life were and how they affected everything. Before then, I had people I looked up to and admired, but they were one, maybe two, dimensional at best. They were good at business but worthless as fathers and husbands. Or they were amazing men of faith, but their health was in shambles, or their finances were disorganized. Why can't you be an amazing dad who is running a successful company, is healthy, and has a marriage on fire, all while building your wealth? Why is this not possible? It is.

The vision was cast, the journey began. I now recognized I had no choice. Once "my direction was set and course known," in the words of Trevor Moawad, I no longer had so many choices, I simply had a set of decisions to make. I could live life on fire, live my health on fire, live a business on fire. I was still missing some pieces that would put this puzzle together, but at least, now I knew and believed living a three-dimensional life was possible. Are you tired of living a one-dimensional life?

Throughout this book you have been given opportunities to make choices, and create awareness in your life. I have shared with you the ones I made, good and bad. If you have chosen to live three-dimensional in your life, the choices of *not* living three-dimensional are gone. They are no longer an option. You simply have a set of decisions to make. Decisions that will lead you to a life on fire!

CHAPTER 9

Swing Batter, Batter

From Paralysis to Peace

We often have big plans, which means we have big projects. Unfortunately, *big* can be paralyzing. How do you go from making hundreds of dollars to hundreds of millions of dollars? How do you go from average to excellence? It's like trying to climb Mt. Everest when you've never climbed before. It seems impossible and absolutely daunting.

Every day that no action is taken, we become another day further away from our goal. We are another day having not accomplished anything significant. Anything worth writing about. Settling into our complacency. Through the instruction of failure and disappointment, I've learned to think smaller, but *not settling* for smaller. I now understand taking an intentional small step, making a small decision for a given direction or goal will lead into more small steps, decisions, and directions; as they multiply, they begin to compound. When that happens, watch out! That's when big things happen!

No One Is Coming to Save You

Throughout my journey, I was always waiting for someone or something—a book, a movie, a song, a mentor—to show up and save me. I couldn't do it on my own. I lacked the skills and the tools. I felt that even if it were possible, it was going to have to come from outside of me.

But no one could save me.

That's a hard truth. Yes, your family can love you through it. Your significant other can support you as much as they know how. And having mentors, like we talked about in the last chapter, is massive. You must remember though: Nobody, *except you*, can save you. Now as a man of faith, I want to clarify that I'm not talking about eternal salvation. I'm referring to saving you from your own dark pit.

We all need to come to a point in our lives where we draw the line in the sand. Where enough is enough, and we start to use our *selfishness* as a means for positive improvement within ourselves. For many of us, we've been selfish with our actions, our choices, with the decisions we've made that simply did not bring true value to ourselves or others. Selfish choices that didn't put others first. Now it's time to rethink what being selfish *in order* to become our best selves, both for others and for ourselves, looks like.

As we look at being selfish with ourselves, we must focus on four areas:

- Developing ourselves.
- Filling our cups.
- Pouring into others.
- Finishing the race.

Developing Yourself

Going back to becoming three dimensional, each one of these dimensions—business, health, and life—requires you to be growing in them, in order to live a life on fire. Being selfish in order to become your best self means being specific and intentional in these most important areas in your life.

Fill Your Cups

Can you identify how you bring passion, fire, and intensity into your life? When your cup is overflowing, what does life look like? These answers need to become a part of you, consistently. In my life, physical fitness fills one of my cups; it is a daily ritual for me. It helps me clear the mechanism and gives the much-needed energy required to perform at my best in life. It also fills my need to "embrace the suck" in my life.

Now that may sound awful so let me explain. While we chased after our massive dreams and goals, we chose many times over to embrace really hard tasks, situations, and challenges in order to pursue and one day accomplish that journey. And while, in the moment, they sucked, were painful, miserable, and sometimes ridiculous, it's those same memories we cling to that bring a smile of satisfaction to our lives. We were *meant* to do hard things! We were created to thrive by putting ourselves through difficult challenges. By intentionally finding the areas in my life where I can create sucky situations and tackle them I create an environment that helps me tackle other challenges that I would normally deflect, ignore or walk away from. Instead, it builds my *grit* muscle, my *take-the-hill* mentality, my *never-give-up* again cry!

According to the most recent census statistics, 39 percent of marriages are ending in divorce. I've always found statistics interesting. They most certainly serve a purpose, but they often don't tell the complete picture. Nor do they give any detail to the hidden possible theme. One must investigate multiple angles and dive deep into what the root causes are behind the statistics.

Divorce is no different. In fact, I believe it is an even more powerful example of why filling our cups is vital to our lives and marriages. Lack of commitment consistently hits the top reasons for divorce. Commitment to what? Commitment to each other, first and foremost, and then to ourselves individually. Filling our personal cups and those of our spouse builds the commitment, the bond. It forges us together, fills the cracks, and adds more "rebar" to our foundations. But like any successful piece in our lives, it must be done intentionally and consistently.

Kate and I realize this and have made the commitment to date night every week. Now that can vary, and there are many different forms, but the one we try to commit to the most is "wine with the wife," which is no doubt my favorite! Every week, we fill our marriage cup by connecting in some intentional way. By doing this, we are always making sure we find our way back to being on the same page, because life pulls us in all different directions.

As I pursue opportunities in business, she continues to pour her heart into our children, manages our home, and helps create a life worth loving. We identify the areas of life that may be challenging for us at that time and communicate with each other on how we are dealing with them. Most of the time, however, we are talking about our hopes and dreams and creating a life with purpose and intent. Every week, Kate and I will also go over how we are spending intentional, quality kid time and family time. Understand, these are *moments*. Often after the boys and I have baseball practice, it's Starbucks and some extra time in the car. It can be letting Grace "do" dad's hair. Or listening to Maddy read me a book.

We overestimate the amount of time and underestimate the *quality* of the time we need to be available. This fills our family and parent cups. I don't know why it took me so long as a father to recognize that this needed to be a cup; I'm embarrassed to admit it actually. Honestly, I felt like everything else I was doing was showing our children how much dad loved them, but it became apparent, in reflection, that I needed to be more intentional in my time with our children.

The last part of filling a cup is about *you* time. As we give so much of ourselves to others, we need to remember ourselves. How are you spending time with just yourself? What are you enjoying with just you? When I adopted this specific action in my life, giving myself permission to spend alone time was one of the greatest gifts I have implemented in my life.

I can already hear it. Seriously? Me time? Alone time? Yes, absolutely! I want you to think of a candle. We spend so much or our time focused on the wax time of our life. Think about this metaphor for a moment. We build and build and build to make our candles the biggest and best they can be. Why? So we can have the baddest freaking flame! But if all we are doing is building the wax and we never focus on the flame, then we've lost our focus. We've lost the heat, the fire in our lives. We've lost *us* . . . again.

This alone time is meant to replenish you, to re-energize you, to set you on fire! So, what should you do? Here's the beauty and the challenge in all of this. Whatever it is for me, it is not for you. And vice versa. You be you! You do what it is that lights your flame. Just do the thing you like to do, regardless of what others feel about it. You must give yourself permission to trust this and to do this. Do not skip filling this cup. Do not let the voices in your head convince you that you are not worth it.

I became important again. And because I became important, I became worthy, confident, and comfortable with myself. I never saw that coming. Never could I have known in advance the power of this change. It's time to find yourself again.

Pour into Others

Next to pouring into your family, there is no better fulfillment than to pass along into someone else your experiences and life lessons. When you find an individual who is willing to learn and adopt the things you are giving, it's such a rewarding experience. When you see a life impacted and changed for the better, it's beyond gratifying—it's legacy worthy.

I remember having a conversation with my father about building a legacy. At that point, I wasn't quite sure who I was supposed to become in my life. I was motivated, but still so uneasy and restless. Not a great combination, and yet certainly able to do some damage! I remember being in a funk about my legacy, or lack thereof.

Once in a while, we are slapped with the realization of our own mortality, our temporality. This happened to me when our community tragically lost an amazing man. He had given of his treasures, his time, his wisdom, his heart. At first, his death reminded me how far I still needed to go to make any kind of impact.

His passing brought forth my insecurity of living a meaningless life. This might sound egotistical, even ridiculous or pathetic, to some, but it's the truth. We compare ourselves to those we admire; it's how we garner some direction of how to live. This community member mentored people with whom he'd never met simply by the way he lived his life. Be that way.

At the time, I was being the best dad and husband I knew how to be, but I felt I could be so much more to so many more. As my dad and I were talking, I spoke pretty freely about this, and receiving his words of wisdom gave me hope.

"Josh, men focus on putting their names on plaques and buildings. In a few generations, most will not remember or know that man or what he did. You have the opportunity to impact a generation, which will then have the ability to impact another generation. Don't try to save the world, and lose your family. Pour into and lead your children, then watch your legacy grow."

This is why you need to have people sitting at your board table. If we allow our thoughts and our emotions to persuade us in the decisions we make before seeking counsel, we miss out on a golden opportunity to avoid misdirection and making the wrong decision.

STRIKE THREE

From that moment on, I've had a renewed sense of conviction as a parent and of my opportunity to be their dad. Don't pass by that word I just used, opportunity. As parents we often see our roles as a duty. And yes, we do have a duty to our children, however when we simply change the word and see what an honor and blessing it is that we have been given we begin to realize the opportunity we have to make true significant impact. When you come to the realization that God does not need you to raise your children but still has called you to do it, it brings a whole new level of respect and dignity to being a parent. To all parents out there, are you pouring into your children? If not, it's time to start.

CHAPTER 10

Casting Your Vision

What Is the Price?

When baseball was done, I didn't know what to do, but like I said in the earlier chapters, I fell into real estate and it would eventually become the next *uniform* I would wear. It was something I could do and become good at. No, I didn't have a passion for the industry. I didn't draw pictures of houses with my name on the for sale sign in front of it in grade school. I simply had no clue what I wanted to do with my life and real estate checked the needed boxes. All I knew was I wasn't going to become a carpenter, like my father, and pound nails the rest of my life. While I gained universal values (work ethic, integrity, honesty, etc.) from watching my dad do this to put food on our table, I knew it wasn't a fit for me.

What I lacked was a vision. In fact, it's hard to believe but no one even asked me what I wanted to do next, or who I wanted to become. There is no debriefing when you hand over your jersey and the transition into your new reality is pretty rough. As I've reflected on this *debriefing*, this *transition*, many times in my life, I understand with absolute clarity that it doesn't have to be done alone.

Never challenged to answer what the vision for my life was, I lived each day narrowly focused on settling in, on staying above water. As I've shared throughout this book, I was always unsettled. Always unfulfilled. There was a huge hole in me that I tried and tried to fill. And even though I was surrounded by amazing, loving people, I needed to find others who I could relate to. I needed to be open about being open. So I searched. As a self-proclaimed entrepreneur, I believed that starting a business, opening an office, or partnering with other people would fill that pit.

I started saying yes to multiple business opportunities, hoping that one of them would give me the purpose I was searching for. What I was doing, in fact, was reaching out to latch onto someone else's purpose. And there is nothing wrong with that, by the way. A dream within a dream is fine. Great visionaries need others to help them make an impact far greater than they could manage on their own.

Though my business partners would help me find passion in my life again, they could not give purpose to my life. Every one of these ventures was about trying to find a deeper meaning in my life—giving purpose to a life that was currently without purpose.

One problem with saying yes to so many business opportunities was that many of them were startups. Being young and inexperienced, I had no idea what it took or how long it could take to even see a profit, or if profit was ever going to happen. Half of small businesses fail within their first five years. Twenty percent, in their first year. Why? Lack of having a plan (that was me). Lack of leadership (another box checked). I had some leadership skills, like enthusiasm, grit, work ethic, passion. These blanket leadership skills gave me enough clout to do nothing more than make some really bad decisions.

Do you find yourself committing to too many things with the hope of finding your vision or purpose? If we do not cast a vision, we end up chasing everything that comes across our path. We soon exhaust ourselves with all the attractions. We've spent months, even years planting seeds, waiting for them to germinate into something much

STRIKE THREE

bigger. Hoping, praying it will turn into a massive oak tree. However, what we have to become aware of is that when the tree starts to sprout, we must then figure out where we need to plant our tree. If we do not have a vision for where we are planting it, one day we'll wake up and realize it was planted next to the landfill, the cemetery, or the trailer park. (Nothing wrong with trailer parks; I know people who are making millions investing in them!)

I know this can be confusing, so let me give a specific example. I became a successful real estate agent but after four years, I needed to move my tree before it got too big to move. As I constantly reviewed my personal and professional goals, and my wife and I, our family goals, we had to make a decision that would set us back financially in order to *move* our tree. Kate wanted to stay at home full-time with the kids, and I wanted to grow myself as a leader and entrepreneur. Our tree was currently planted and the foundation seemed very solid. But because we had a vision, because we continued to raise the expectations of how we could live as a family, we moved our tree and started to build a bigger and much deeper foundation. Together we decided our family was more important than the income from Kate's job. So Kate stayed home for our families needs. I started to phase out of actively selling. Two massive decisions made because of the vision we had for our future. The roots have become bigger, stronger, deeper, and wider. And now the fruits of those decisions we made years ago are starting to bloom in our lives.

It's impossible to stay focused or be truly courageous if you don't have your eyes set on anything.

The vision for my life's purpose has come through more soul searching, more questioning and chasing, more discouragement, more conversations, more testing, more God-talks than I could ever have imagined. The wisdom gained through these experiences has shaped me, refined me, and convicted me to take ownership of what I believe I'm being called to do. But more importantly, whom I am being called to serve?

So how do you discover your purpose? Simple, yet not easy. One of my favorite speakers is Andy Stanley. At the time of this book, Andy is the senior pastor of North Point Community Church. He founded North Point Ministries and has written over 22 books. His leadership podcast, The Andy Stanley Leadership Podcast is one of the most popular leadership podcasts and definitely one of my top recommendations. When it comes to purpose, Andy would argue as follows:

Your purpose can be found on the other side of, *what's in it for me?* Your purpose will be found when you can say no to yourself and yes to something bigger than yourself. Purpose is about becoming the "means" in order to get to the end, not to be the end. How will you serve others? Are you willing to pay the price? Your purpose will be found when the burden you feel, meets the opportunity you see, with the skill that you have.

Read that last sentence again. What's your burden? What's your skill? What's the opportunity you see? When you recognize that *thing* in your life that makes you ache, makes you stay up late, get up early, causes you to crave more and more and more of it, then you've found your purpose. Now the real journey to realize how you can live it out can begin.

When you are able to say yes to this question:
Am I willing to pay the price for my purpose?
Then your journey can begin.

A Vision for Your Life

Suddenly, you matter again. A vision makes you an important link between your current life and what can be.

A vision for your life will provide the motivation you've been searching for. When you see the picture of what could be, even the mundane things seem rousing. When you catch a glimpse of a future life, it gives you direction. That focus on your vision keeps you from limiting your options by being distracted and just drifting through your days.

The key here is to find a purpose that will actually fulfill you. Andy Stanley describes purpose as a "... means to an end. I want to know my purpose, so I won't be without purpose." Nobody wants to be without purpose. Unfortunately, very few people end up where they are in life, *on* purpose!

We can become paralyzed by not making a simple decision to move forward. Perhaps you don't know the correct next steps or decision to be made. It's easy to feel overwhelmed from past failures, and not choose to take the next step. And yet, when you don't create any momentum, you can become disheartened by the lack of progress in your life, falling into an endless cycle.

We have a tendency to falsely believe there is only one path, one direction in order to get to where we need to go. That's why we've been hung up on the past. The bridge blew up, the road was destroyed, and the path became unclear, confusing and overgrown with so much garbage, baggage, and false stories. Sink this next statement into your mind. *There are endless paths in life, focusing and finding a path you can confidently walk is where we are aiming.* The vision for your life becomes refined along the way, thus you will be refined along the journey. Though you need to begin with the end in mind, understand the end is not written in stone!

Your Story Is Yours

This book isn't just about finding our way. It's much more than that—it's about your ability to step up and take action. I know you can do it and I want to help. Just as my story is written on these pages, your story is written into your heart. Your path has not been perfect, but it was perfectly planned for you. Your story is yours and yours alone. It is unique and powerful! Your message is yours to be shared for others, to be strength for others.

This book was written because of the many men and women who have poured their hearts out into books, teachings, and conversations that have inspired and strengthened me. I have been the recipient not because they know me but because I searched for them. My life has been forever changed and my vision made clear, because of those who stepped out before me and gave me courage to realize I was not alone. It is because of these people that you are reading this.

So, what will you do with it now? How will you cast your vision of your life and become an impact on others? How will you discover the burden you feel, with the skills you have and the opportunity you see?

It's time to get off the sidelines. It's time to move.

CHAPTER 11

Designed through Failure

You Have One Life to Live

On the day I signed my contract to play professional baseball, I was in Grand Junction, Colorado. Home to the Junior College World Series. Having just pitched one of the best games of my career to that point, my position as a second-round draftee for the Colorado Rockies was solidified. My former high school pitching coach, Alex Neeley, helped my father and me negotiate the signing bonus and structure my contract.

Alex, a former minor league pitcher himself, taught me the curve ball, the pitch that played an integral part in my career. However, one of the most impactful things Alex did was inspire me through the vivid pictures he painted of a life in minor league baseball. His stories brought this surreal world to life. He lit up our young minds with stories upon stories before we could even fathom them in our own dreams.

Now, much like the days in high school, our destination may be hundreds of miles away, or it could be just around the corner. You may still feel so lost during this time and you don't know where to begin the journey. Well, you're in chapter 11 of this book; you've already started the journey. Be proud of that and take another step. Take another chance.

Because we lived at such a high level of expectation and commitment when chasing that other dream, we understand the concept of *doing* the work. We know that work needs to be done and sacrifices need to be made. We know that a price needs to be paid. It's not a matter of whether we need to do it—it's a matter of *what* we need to do and *why* we are doing it. We always knew the *why* before. We were always secure in that.

You now realize your past does not define you, it actually *refines* you. You now know just how incredibly unique and gifted you are, and realize you can't settle. Isn't it amazing to think that *your* life, through *your* failures, was designed to bring out your best self?

The True Game

I see my life through two perspectives. On one hand, I've experienced some incredible memories and opportunities. Every day, I am intentional with pursuing my purpose in one form or another, pushing to grow myself and pour into others. I'm pouring into myself and the people around me. I have more clarity in my life than I've ever had, and because of that, I have more peace in my life.

On the other hand, I see how small I'm playing. I see how many times I don't stay focused on pushing for the bigger opportunity. I see how I've settled in areas of my life and how much more I need to grow and learn. I see how scared I can play in life and how I can live with so much more boldness and conviction. However, I no longer live in scarcity; I have identified my purpose.

For years after baseball, I would have a vibrant dream over and over again. I was playing centerfield. (Why the heck I was playing centerfield? I have no idea.) The temperature was perfect, the sky was dark, and the lights shined bright on the fluorescent green grass. The players were all at their positions, though I didn't recognize any of them. Our uniforms were all clad in generic white with black trim. It was reminiscent of the movie Field of Dreams. The lights shined on the seats, but the stadium was empty of fans. As the pitcher threw the ball, I took my stance and prepared for the play. The ball was hit and headed toward me. Every detail was vivid, and my mind visualized the entire play, from the route I would take, to the glove opening up to catch the ball in stride.

As I began to move toward the ball, nothing worked. My body wasn't reacting to what my mind was telling it to do. My body wouldn't freakin' move! The resistance was so powerful, no matter how hard I tried, I couldn't get my limbs to react. The game was still coming full speed all around me, and all I could do was watch it pass by. This dream would continue to haunt me; I would wake up nervous, pissed, and confused. Why would I have the same dream repeatedly in my life? Through the many years it took to discover myself again, I came to realize these dreams were manifesting my fears of a life passing me by.

When I finally came face-to-face with myself and made the decision to take back ownership of my life, the dreams went away. When I discovered myself, reinvented my new self, the dreams disappeared. I was no longer living in scarcity.

The real game had begun!

Be More

So how do I live out my purpose, you may be wondering. When I read an author in whom I'm interested, listen to their podcast, or watch a video that they created, I always want to know more about the daily activities in their life. I want to know the specifics of what they are actually doing and how they are living out their purpose. What organizations have they built? What meetings do they attend or run? What conversations are they having? I want to know this so I can imitate their actions. I want to replicate the activities, the structure they created, in order to live out an exceptional life. But most importantly, I want to know what burden they have discovered is buried in them. I want to know the talent they unlocked and how they saw their opportunity come from it all.

As I faced life after baseball, I know how broken I became. I remember the stories, the lies I would tell myself and own. I remember the hopelessness I felt. The burden I discovered was the overwhelming emotion of fear, uncertainty, failure, and doubt that we face when the chase is over. And then we realize we don't have the tools to build a life from there.

Something has to be done. You and I have a duty and an obligation to do more and to be more for ourselves and those around us. More specifically, we have an obligation to become all they were created to become. The opportunity awaits us if we choose to fight for it. My biggest revelations came from powerful moments of self-discovering, intentional situations of doing hard shit. All with an intent of finding my greater purpose.

Men listen up. Men need other men as mentors, friends and brothers. Throughout this book, I have preached leadership and the importance of leading in our lives. And while this is still very much true, we must also have the humility to sit at another man's feet. To listen to advice, to hear feedback and take ownership of that feedback. I've been blessed to have had a few great men in my life, my father at the top of the list. My dad leads with the conviction to be all he was created to be. My father has been a great example of what a *real* man looks like.

Unfortunately, our society has depicted men to be dumb, insignificant, irrelevant, even useless. Remember that TV series, *Married with Children*? The dad was the bumbling idiot in front of the TV all the time. We *can't* let these portraits of manhood paint our idea of what we are. As a country, we are facing many challenges; the lack of men stepping up as fathers is the leading source of our issues. Fathers need to step up. Husbands need to lead up. Men need to **rise up**! As a society, we've lost our way in knowing what a man's role is. It's time to take back that role.

So what do you do if this movement doesn't exist? You create it. Kingsmen was created from all the experiences I went through in order to find myself. It never started as an *accelerator* for other men, or an organization that would help men get out of their pit, bridge the gap, and take back their headship. It was about fixing me, figuring me out. Helping *me* discover *me* again. But once I saw what it did for myself, it became a bigger vision to see what God's greater purpose was meant for.

The name *Kingsmen* would come from our history books and the mighty men of King David. As early as King David, men have been drawn together for strength, for wisdom, for victory. The thirty mighty men of King David were brought together by a bond to protect each other and to serve each other for a greater purpose, a greater vision. That vision and calling needs to be uncovered again. I believe that men want to rise up in their lives. Men want to step up as fathers and as husbands, and they want to *be the man*! But most of us are not equipped with the tools, the know-how, the direction, or the support to do it. The mission of Kingsmen is to create a brotherhood of men who embody, live out and challenge themselves to achieve excellence in their lives.

God exposed my burden, showed me what I was being called to do, and now He just needed me to step out in faith and to follow His lead. Thus, Kingsmen was born. Through our events and our private network, men are discovering everything they were meant to be, all while creating the bonds and brotherhood they've been searching for.

Give It Your All

Here is one of the principles of Kingsmen:

0% left.
Empty the tank.
Every day in Every way.

To waste your time is to waste your life. To master your time is to master your life. I don't know about you but I want to go to bed exhausted. I want to rest my head on the pillow knowing I gave all I could that day. Regardless of victory or failure, I want to fall asleep exhausted by the effort and passion I gave. There are many days when I don't accomplish everything I challenge myself to do. However, because I live each day with intentionality, my days are filled with a mindset of what I *get* to do in order to find fulfillment in my life. I still have to do the hard stuff, uncomfortable stuff, required-by-the-job-description stuff. But my life is not overrun with the "have to do's." I'm designing my day; I'm creating my life.

Can you say this about your life? Is your day structured around the "have to's" or "get to's"? Is your day reactive or proactive? Is your day designed or auto-filled?

Now understand, I'm not perfect. Many are the days when life gets in the way and my day spins out of control; however, that's where this thing called grace comes in. It's a constant battle to show myself grace. They are many times when I need to stand back from the moment and just breathe, relax and refocus on what I can control. I'm also learning to master my inner voice and the way I speak to myself.

Have you ever thought about how much authority you give away in your life? How much ownership do we take from what others think or say about us? Reality check, no one owns you. No one can make you think one thing or the other. No one can make you react to a situation without your consent. You have the power to be strong and resilient. Stop wasting time on the distractions created by others and start mastering your headspace and the personal authority given to you in order to create a life you're proud to live.

STRIKE THREE

What do you think your life would look like if you decided to go all in? What would happen if you took the simple action steps in this book and *actually* started to live them out?

What if you embraced your pit and opened your black box? Forgave yourself and forgave others? Took back the 1%? Embraced the suck? Moved your finish line? Created a board of mentors? Started small? Filled your cups? Filled the cups of others? Trusted the process? Showed up everyday in your life? And never gave up?

What if you did all of that?

Our lives are a reflection of what we've created through the struggles we've embraced. The choices we've made. The failures we've experienced. A combination of everything we've accepted and put up with. You've been through the fire and your shell has been cracked open. The seed that was planted years ago has been germinating and has begun to grow. Plant the tree, let the foundation take root.

In order to be all that you were created to be, you must become the person you never thought you could. It's time to grow.

Draw the Line in the Sand

Throughout my journey, the challenges became more difficult and the conversations more intense. When we come to the heavy conclusion we can be more than we are, a new wave of responsibility splashes upon the shores of our consciousness. We also feel these new challenges differently, and the failures cut deeper. Once I knew *why* I was going to go through all of it, that helped ease the burden. We need to make sure we have God as our beacon in what can become a very rough sea.

Don't let the fear of the unknown stop you from moving. I get it, I know the reason you don't want to make the move. It may feel like it moves you backwards. But that's okay because it's only temporary. You have to pull a slingshot back before it can launch. There are many paths to get you where you want to go. I never realized this. Nobody ever told me, "Just move. It's okay to fail again. You are stronger than your failures." I had to discover this for myself on my journey. But it wasn't until I started pouring back into the lives of others that I began to see why everything I'd gone through was exactly what I *needed* to go through.

My past has made me who I am today. Not just because of my past, but because I'm choosing to embrace my past and use it for something far greater than myself. I am choosing to not repeat it. I'm choosing to help others with it. I'm choosing to be the "means" *not* the end.

It's an intimidating proposition no doubt, but you must decide. Let me share with you a secret: It doesn't matter. Really, it doesn't matter. Just make a decision. Have some discernment before you do, but decide and go with it.

One misconception is that after all this self-discovery, after finding all these tools, strategies, and self-awareness, my life is perfect. I know when I read or listen to people whom I admire and see their success, I imagine their lives being flawless, or at least devoid of everyday problems. Let me set the record straight and say how ridiculously imperfect I am.

Each battle exposes an angle of weakness in me, in us, and because of that, we must make a choice to stand and fight. You must draw a line in the sand of your life. There can be no retreat at this point. The old version of us would have retreated, but this time, we are different. This time we know we must stay and walk the line. This *is* our time! This *is* our moment!

There are days, I can be wound up pretty tight as I battle my unhealthy beast, the beast of failure and scarcity. There are days when I don't stay in my disciplines. There are times when I am apologizing to Kate for my lack of patience, or my frustration from one thing or another. But there's a difference in my life now which affirms my direction. I acknowledge my mistakes and actually make a change. Action. I take action and become proactive. I choose to make a stand.

You have chosen to take a stand and prepare for battle; now things have changed. It's only a metaphor, but real battles are upon us. Unlike before, these challenges must be faced. This is when you discover yourself. This is when you recreate yourself.

There Is No One Thing

I must admit most of the books I read are from well-known, well-established, successful people who have a platform. However, the ones I love to find are from authors who, I believe, are just like me, out there grinding to make that life and impact. Any person who is pushing every day to reach

STRIKE THREE

their next level. They had a dream or a vision and put it all on the line. Who despite having no odds (like if the odds were stacked against them, at least they'd have some odds), still chose to put their faith between themselves and their fear. We can often exclude our faith when it comes to overcoming the obstacles we face. Faith bridges the gap and gives courage to dream bigger, chase harder, and challenge greater. I see myself in them, and that gives me hope. It gives me courage to dream a dream only God can deliver. We all need more courage in our life.

As I sit in my office writing this last chapter, I look around our company's walls, thinking of the people we lead, the lives we are a part of that have been impacted by the vision and execution of something much bigger than ourselves. The walls around me have changed quite a bit; however, the walls inside me are the ones that have changed the most. As life shapes our thoughts, decisions and outlooks it becomes very natural to build up walls within us for protection. Unfortunetly, many times they hold us back from taking that chance, creating that business, asking that question, dreaming that dream. Before, all I could see were my walls spray painted with the graffiti of disappointment and failure. I had to break down those walls! Looking around now, all I see is potential, opportunity, and exciting new challenges. You, too, are capable of breaking your walls.

I look at situations with excitement and determination to create a better life, and yet, I feel so blessed with my current life. Not content, but not anxious. Not settling, and yet I have peace. I love my life, but still work hard because it can be better, I can be so much better! In fact, I would say my ambitions are much bigger than ever. This may all seem contradictory, but in truth, what you need to take from this book is this: Find the awareness that what you're working to do has value, where you are right now has value, and where you want to be has value.

Regardless of what direction you take, you need tools to help get you there. Here are a few of my favorite ones.

Begin the journal: There are many reasons why a journal is a powerful resource. Journals help by giving the ability to self-reflect, provide clarity on what your emotions are telling you, to let out frustration, and give celebration. It's a place to let yourself be human. Another aspect of the journal is that it becomes a legacy you leave for others. You never know when the day will come that you're called back home.

I want my journal to be a place where my family can go to read the pages of my life. The thoughts I didn't share, the challenges I faced, but more importantly the joy I had, the happiness I experienced, and the love I had for life. I want my wife to know how often I thought of her. I want for my children to know how much I loved them as well as knowing that everything I did had their names on it. My journal is a reflection of the true man I desired to be and the man I tried to become. Begin your journal.

Change it up: Far too many of us are told to set long-term goals. So we set long-term ideas, and we don't look at the smaller quicker wins we could accomplish. It's about the pebbles. It's so important to set thirty-day challenges; heck, set weekly and daily challenges. In order to make massive changes in your life, you need to create momentum. If you don't experience some instant wins, it's extremely hard to stay focused and motivated.

You must make weekly wins, daily wins, small wins a part of your schedule. It could be a weekly date night, daily workouts, daily "me" time. I personally like to make boxes and check them off. I may have a goal for three daily thank-you cards. There's something powerful and satisfying about simply checking off the boxes. As a high achiever, for us, the wins—every win—are important. Do not underestimate the small wins.

Bring others with you: Many of the experiences you need to go through require you to do them alone, but not all of them. Who can you bring along for the journey? I need to clarify something important here. These are not people sitting at your board table. These are not the people who have a seat at your table. Ask yourself the following questions. Are there people in your life right now that could be impacted by your story? Are there people in your life that could experience healing if you shared your struggle? Part of the healing process for yourself will be to pour into others. As Andy Stanley says, "Who could you be the *means* to?"

As I've shared, so much of my healing came from having to take ownership of my past, forgiving myself for the "old" me and my "old" ways. But the deeper healing came when I knew I could pour into others. Who can you bring with you?

Start living: When the career was over, so was life as we knew it. We stopped being adventurous, we stopped pushing ourselves to extreme and uncomfortable levels. Wake up and start *living* again! Find something that challenges you and makes you commit to a high level of achievement. For me, it began with Spartan races. But it won't stop there. I continue to hunt for other sources of leaving (or being pushed out of) my comfort zone, to push myself to experience anxiety and victory. That's what we miss. We often fantasize about how great the past was, when in reality: It was high stress, high anxiety, high emotions, high failure *and* high success simultaneously.

Go find it again. Run a 5K, compete in a triathlon, take up a sport. Whatever it is, do it for you. Start with a team or group of people, if possible. One of the emotions we miss most is the bond we experience with teammates. Having others we can encourage, support, and help cross the finish line gives us that feeling we've missed and longed for. You need to find others who will *push and pull* you in ways that you can't. Promise yourself you'll do this. If you want to start living at a level that sets you on fire then buck up! Commit to the journey, commit to the challenge and start living!

Find high performers: Nothing will help you reach greater levels of success than being in the presence of high achievers. Who cares what they are great at, make them a part of your life. Have coffee with them. Take them to lunch. Make it a monthly appointment. Be an avid learner in the presence of high performers. Learn from them what you can and then implement it into your life. You may find that you aren't friends with these people, but it's more of a mentor/mentee type relationship. If they're willing to enter into this type of deal, don't feel bad; they have something you need. Remember back when I said how crucial it is to pour into others? They know this same importance; be glad they're willing to pour into you!

Pay to play: If you truly want to grow to a level you never thought you could or tap into potential you always knew you wanted to discover then ask yourself this question: What price am I willing to pay? Not an emotional or physical price; that's easy. Are you willing to invest financially? Because if you are not, then why would anyone else invest in you? I learned that my future success was going to be tied directly to the amount of money I was willing to invest into myself. Some of my greatest achievements, insights, friendships and breakthroughs came because of a mentor or a coach that I invested in. And I continue to see the value. I'm paying to play; will you?

Throughout this book, I've asked a ton of questions. You want to grow, ask questions. You want to become someone greater than you are today, ask good questions. You want to be the person you desire to be, ask the right questions. This takes practice, this takes intent. When I first started to ask questions, I was terrible at it. In fact, I was so bad I decided to purchase books that taught me what questions I should be asking. See my 25 best questions in our resource guide at www.joshkalinowski.com.

Fill yourself daily: I spoke earlier on how important it is to be selfish with yourself. I'm addressing it again because it is that important.

STRIKE THREE

Filling your cup, taking care of yourself, and staying in your disciplines are the keys to finding yourself again and finding that happiness you've been chasing. You will only set your life on fire when *you* are ablaze!

As I look back on what I needed in my life, it can be overwhelming to think about all the insecurities I had, the shame I felt, the fear I let control my life. I used so many distractions to dull the noise and the truth. When I changed what I filled myself with, how I took care of myself, and how I stayed in my disciplines, I changed.

If you want to change the person you have become, start with what you fill yourself with. When the pressure squeezes, everything you've put inside eventually comes out. So, what do you want to come out? Start acting like the person you desire to be and soon enough you will be that person. I know my vision, I know my purpose, I know me.

It's your time: As your eyes take in the final words of this book, realize that your next chapters are yet to be written. You have opened the pages to a new life. Take the pen and take charge! You have been given this amazing gift called life. And because of that, you have an obligation and a duty to live it out courageously! Find that power inside you again and focus on it. Let that power consume you. Let it set you on fire again. Become relentless again. Become unapologetic again. Become worthy of greatness again. Because . . . you are worthy. You are worthy. YOU ARE WORTHY!

> *"For I know the plans I have for you, declares the Lord,*
> *plans to prosper you and not to harm you,*
> *plans to give you hope and a future."*
> Jeremiah 29:11

You are stronger because of your failures.
It's time to make *your* move.
Love and Life,
-JK

Acknowledgment

There is no way I could end without thanking the many people that inspired, listened, read, talked and prayed for me and this book. This experience has been a labor of love, including frustration, doubt, exhaustion, joy, triumph, and victory. But like any worthy accomplishment, it is what I learned through the journey that has left me the most impactful lessons.

To all the coaches who put up with my antics, my tantrums and my infamous facial expressions, thank you! Thank you for not giving up on me. For inspiring me to be better and become my best. You made an impact in my life, taught me valuable lessons and are a reason I am able to write this book. I'd like to especially thank the coaches who helped shape me and my career. The entire NC Mustang coaching staff, Alex Neely and the American Legion Coaching staff, Cam Walker and the coaching staff at Indian Hills Community College, Rick Matthews Pitching Coordinator for the Colorado Rockies organization, Ron Gideon Manager for the Colorado Rockies organization, Bob McClure Pitching Coach for the Colorado Rockies organization. Each one of you in one form or another, through a conversation or belief in me, helped discover the man I wanted to become. Though it has taken years to uncover, you played a significant role in helping me discover me!

To the many inspiring mentors in my life (whether you know it or not!), your daily words and books fill my cup and motivate me to keep chasing my lions! You challenge my status quo and help me raise the standard by which I live my life. Thank you Sharran Srivatsaa, Todd Conklin, Ed Mylett, Andy Frisella, Bedros Keuillian, John C. Maxwell, Fr. Mike Schmitz, Marc Batterson, Patrick Lencioni, Andy Stanley, Craig Groeschel, Brian Buffini, Ken Coleman and countless others I'm sure I missed. Thank you for shaping me and my mindset!

To my extraordinary wife Kate, thank you for your unwavering support. The many nights with the bedroom lights on as I would write into the late hours and you would try to fall asleep. The encouragement to never let me stop, even when the frustration was at its highest. But most importantly never giving up on me as I journeyed, discover and reinvented myself over all these years. Our marriage is a product of your faithfulness. Love you more than I can express, but know I will spend the rest of my life trying to…

To my amazing children, never stop dreaming. Never let anyone tell you that you can't. Believe in yourself and the potential that you have inside. Know that it is through the challenges, disappointments and losses that we will discover our greatest achievements and purpose. Know that your mom and I will always be your biggest fans! Go chase your lions!

To my parents. Your patience throughout my life has empowered me to discover the wonderful meaning of grace and unwavering love. I always knew how much I was loved even when I didn't feel worthy of it. You always had my back and walked alongside so many of my disappointments. You inspire me to be the parents you were and continue to be. Your support is written through the pages of my life. Thank you.

Thank you to all of my Kingsmen, friends, family and business associates. Your encouragement and words of wisdom fill my cup and helped me stay the course.

Lastly, this book would have no lasting meaning if the message of a loving Father does not resonate in these pages. It was in my darkest times that I felt His presence, His peace and comfort. Though I wasn't always faithful on my end His faithfulness never ceased. It is because of His continued grace and love that I am on this amazing journey today. Thank you Lord for ALL you have done and continue to do in my life…

Love,
A man of *thee* King
– JK